Tracing Our Footsteps:
Fifteen Tales of Hope, Struggle, and Triumph

A   M E M O I R

Wei Wei

Dear Virginia,

To your health.

Your friend.

Wei Wei 6-1-2013

Copyright © 2013 by Wei Wei
First Edition – March 2013
Library and Archives Canada Cataloguing in Publication
Wei, Wei, 1952-
Tracing our footsteps : fifteen tales of hope, struggle, and
triumph: a memoir / Wei Wei.

Includes bibliographical references.
Issued also in electronic format.
ISBN 978-1-4602-0725-3 (bound).--
ISBN 978-1-4602-0726-0 (pbk.)

1. Wei, Wei, 1952- --Family. 2. Wei, Yong Da. 3. Chinese
Americans--Biography. 4. Fathers and daughters--United
States--Biography. 5. Daughters--Family relationships--
United States--Biography. 6. Adult children of immigrants-
-Family relationships--United States--Biography. 7.
Immigrant families--United States--Biography. I. Title.

HQ755.85.W34 2012   306.874092   C2012-907134-X

ISBN
978-1-4602-0725-3 (Hardcover)
978-1-4602-0726-0 (Paperback)
978-1-4602-0727-7 (eBook)

Produced by:

FriesenPress

Suite 300 – 852 Fort Street
Victoria, BC, Canada V8W 1H8
www.friesenpress.com

Distributed to the trade by The Ingram Book Company

Table of Contents

Praise for *Tracing Our Footsteps*

Tracing Our Footsteps offers poignant reflections on the vastly changed worlds of a daughter and her father after decades of separation. Wei draws in readers with engaging first generation stories of coming to the United States as a student juxtaposed with her father's visits as a widow. Each tale weaves distinct moments in their lives through the contexts of diaspora, social change and loss. Food is a critical element of connection and, yet, cultural differences within families. Their conversations reveal complex relations with, at times, raw emotional landscapes of cultural and personal transformation. The paths that both take in forging new lives offer insights onto steps taken to embrace and maintain family bonds. This touching memoir explores the past to illustrate how to savor the present and celebrate significant pleasures of walking, talking, and being together. — Nancy N. Chen, Professor of Anthropology, University of California, Santa Cruz. She is the author of *Breathing Spaces: Qigong, Psychiatry,* and *Healing in China* and of *Food, Medicine,* and *the Quest for Good Health.*

Wei Wei's memoir, *Tracing Our Footsteps: Fifteen Tales of Hope, Struggle, and Triumph*, is both a daughter's tribute to her beloved father and a thoughtful reflection on her own adoption of U.S. culture following immigration from China. Along the way she struggles with what it means to be a "good daughter" (taking care of her parents and family), what flexibility is required to coexist between two such different cultures, how to truly help a beloved parent cope with the loss of a life-long partner, and how to understand her father's personal history in the context of Chinese political history. At times compelling, the book is thought-provoking, sensitive, and loving. Many of the questions it raises about cultural values, relationships, duty, and personal growth would serve as excellent starting points for book club discussions or for advanced high school and college courses. — Ann Koopman, Former *JEFFLINE* Editor, Thomas Jefferson University

A moving memoir that relates the close bond between father and daughter on their journeys through life in China and America ... this honest account of the hopes, struggles and triumphs in their eventful lives is presented in a forthright manner with deep feeling. I was very touched by the emotion underlying these recollections, and inspired by the determination and courage shown by both father and daughter in pursuing their paths in life. — Constance Lim, Editor of *A Singapore Life*

For her recent *Tracing Our Footsteps*, Wei Wei sets the hard, cold steel of life upon her anvil. Her hammer is integrity with which she fashions a series of narratives that both affirm without being sentimental and submerge us in depths profound. She has managed to chronicle lives (her own included) by maintaining a distance that only enhances perspective. By the end of her memoir we feel that she has included us in a journey that was as complex, painful, and as joyful and rewarding as any journey we could hope to take. Thus we are thankful that she has invited us. In this work, we accompany someone who has not only had the experience but also gained the meaning from particular experiences that she has been able to universalize. — Dr. R.F. McEwen, Professor of English and Humanities, Chadron State College, Chadron, NE

This memoir is a fast and enjoyable read that I highly recommend. I was quickly caught up in the story, which is really three stories in one: a touching and personal story of a father, daughter, and granddaughter getting reaquainted; a story about the immigration experience across two generations; and a story about growing up in communist China across two generations. The fifteen tales that are told truly are ones of hope, struggle and triumph. The writing is touching and all the emotions come through in vivid fashion. The stories are universal and easily relateable, and are told in a very compelling style. The frequent flashes of humor in the story telling fit nicely, and makes the overall poignancy of the tales that much more heartfelt. For me, the hidden gem in the memoir are the stories about growing up in communist China for both the author and her father. I found these portions of the memoir to be especially enlightening. These stories were not told in a dry, history book way, but rather in a way that presented life in communist China both tangible and real. I wish that this memoir was made available to me when I was taking history and social studies classes. It makes the world and multiculturalism much more readily understandable. — Catherine Soehner, Librarian, University of Utah

For my daughter, Celine, who was born in America, unaware of her grandpa's past. It is my hope that, as an adult, Celine will one day be strong and courageous in her personal journey in searching for meaning in her life.

In memory of
Patricia Neudorf and Rong Hua Shi
for their bravery, compassion,
kindness, unconditional love, and acceptance.

Grandma

As I look at the stars in the night
I see a glimmer of light oh so bright
And I feel your comfort on me
I know you are there
Rejoicing in heaven
Watching me down here
In the world
Why? Why did you leave me?
Why? Why did you leave?
I miss you
I miss you
I know you are there
Rejoicing in heaven
Watching me down here
In the world
You are always here
With me
You are always here
With Me
- by Celine W. Neudorf

in memory of Celine's grandmother,
Patricia Neudorf, April 21, 1921 – February 14, 2011

Introduction

In February 2004, nearly three years after his wife passed away, Yong Da, my father, embarked upon the journey of his life to America. Aged and broken-hearted, Dad was trying to pick up the pieces and joined me in California looking for a new beginning. Would he be able to embrace this land of freedom and reside permanently on foreign soil?

Tracing Our Footsteps: Fifteen Tales of Hope, Struggle, and Triumph, my memoir, provides a fresh look at the immigrant experience through the lens of a new wave of migration from China to America. When I left China for the pursuit of higher education in the United States, Dad was a middle-aged man who had barely survived the ravages of Chinese wars and political turmoil. Before pursuing a degree in the U.S., I was a young college lecturer in Beijing, and fresh out of school. Later I emigrated to the U.S. in 1981 and ended up in California. During my years of absence from Beijing I occasionally visited home and exchanged letters and phone calls with Dad. In return, my parents paid a brief visit to me in California in the early 1990s. By the time Dad and I were reunited again in the States in 2004, I was a middle-aged woman who had settled down into my daily life as a wife, a mother, and a seasoned faculty member in academia.

From 2004 to 2008, Dad lived with my husband, my daughter, and I at our California central coast home. Since this book is about my efforts to help Dad to fit into a new environment and to re-establish our relationship, I structured it into fifteen tales, focusing on ordinary but profound experiences that Dad and I shared, reflecting upon our personal values, perspectives, and priorities during a five-year period. Much of the book is based on our daily conversations during strolls in our neighborhood after supper. In a process of helping Dad to adapt to the American lifestyle, I retraced my past and memorable events that had taken place in China when I was a child and in my adulthood in America. At the same time, I was thirsty to find out about Dad's story that I was vaguely aware of, but had never been told directly. Through this string of fifteen events, we reconnected and rediscovered ourselves. As I was learning more about Dad, I realized that although we belonged to different generations, our life sagas were not completely isolated, but very much intertwined. Dad's journey to America had made an impact on me, had evoked my own personal experience of searching for the meaning in my life, and had changed me forever.

This book is filled with real-life adventures in the past and the present that offer the reader insight into the life and struggle of a contemporary immigrant family. Today's immigrants arrive from all parts of the world. The book not only tells a story about immigrants, but also tells an American story – a story of a journey shared regardless of age, race, gender, or cultural background.

Out of deep respect, several names throughout this book have been altered for various reasons. The timeframes for certain historical events occurring in Dad's life recorded in this

book may be slightly different than the actual timeframes of
the events.

1. Land of Opportunity

We had arrived at the San Francisco airport just about ten minutes before Dad's plane was scheduled to land. The airport terminal, a facility shared by all international airlines, was crowded on this last Saturday of February 2004. Airports always get me excited, international airports most of all. My excitement comes from hearing different sounds of language and being a part of a place filled with people from all parts of the world. An airport often marks a beginning of a great adventure, as well as (for someone else) a final destination. It produces a dynamic synergy that stimulates feelings of one's connections to the entire universe.

Ironically, I am not fond of air traveling. As I get older, my fear of flying grows stronger, even though statistics show that flying is still safer than driving. However, for me it is more of a control issue. While driving I am more or less in control of the wheels. The car is in my own hands. As a responsible driver, I watch out and try to avoid any bad drivers and their irresponsible behavior on the road. I trust my instincts and try to control my own destiny on the contrary. I don't feel in control while I am in the air. There is an unknown factor up there. Simply, a plane is operated by a stranger. On the ground I am able to appreciate views of trees, rivers, lakes, and mountains. In the air I often find myself staring at huge cotton balls of clouds that block the view of Earth from the sky. I feel sandwiched into a box on a plane.

A red headline dazzled and flashed repeatedly on a wide TV monitor near the arrival gate. The electrons on the screen were reporting the status of arriving planes. A new announcement had just popped up: Air China Flight 985 from Beijing was on time. Near the gate exit, we found a comfortable spot and sat down to wait. Terry, my husband, removed the Saturday newspaper he had been holding underneath one of his arms, unfolded and smoothed it out, and started reading. Our daughter, Celine, was busy playing Sims on her new Game Boy. I leaned over and quickly glanced at the newspaper in Terry's hands. A headline caught my eye, "Professor Eric Kool discusses DNA molecule built in Stanford's lab." That sounded interesting, but I was in no mood to explore it further. I was too restless and constantly checked on the monitor, afraid of missing any update information on Dad's flight. A flight from Tokyo had arrived; flights from Frankfurt and Germany had just landed; Air France from Paris was still on time. All my attention was focused on the dazzling flight numbers reported endlessly on the screen. These red lights were turning and changing constantly, as if they were turning into a fiberglass horse on a merry-go-round in an amusement park; when you ride on it, your head spins. Today it was impossible for me to be calm and hide my feeling of joy. I had not seen Dad since mom had passed away more than two years ago. I was so looking forward to catching up with him, so eager to find out any details and gaps that I had missed since I left him in Beijing in 2001. Today was an important date for both us. Supposedly Dad was going to get his Green Card at the U.S. Immigration Office at the San Francisco airport upon his arrival. He was going to stay with me and my family, hopefully, to rebuild his life in America as a new immigrant.

Flight 985 had just landed on the runway and was gradually gliding towards the arrival gate outside. Dad's plane was on time. Inside the crowd got denser in the waiting area. I suggested that Terry and Celine remain in their seats, while I stood up and walked towards the arrival exit, where incoming passengers would appear. I stopped in front of a rope that divided the exit from the waiting area. There was already a dense line of people waiting at the rope. I managed to squeeze my body in between two large men wearing dark suits standing in front. They did not complain about my intruding. Judging from their serious and official looks, I wondered if they were hired by certain Silicon Valley startups. They wore name tags and were holding a sign made from cardboard with the names of people from a company they were waiting for. I suppose the startups had sent their representatives or drivers to greet their international clients. People had started piling up behind me. In thirty minutes I was going to see Dad again, or so I thought.

The passengers from Flight 985 started popping out one by one, or in small groups, like a parade marching through the gate. These new arrivals were either dragging their suitcases or pushing their airport-rental carts loaded with luggage and other personal belongings moving towards the waiting crowd. At this point Celine and Terry finally abandoned their chairs and joined me to watch the parade passing by. For these passengers, San Francisco was either the end of their journey or was just another temporary stop before moving on to their next adventure. The long, over-night flight didn't seem to affect their mood. Soon after spotting their loved ones or friends, some had thrown their arms in the air, while others greeted each other with tears, hugs, and kisses. Standing beside me, the same dark-suited men each welcomed two strangers with formal hand shakes, then grabbed their suitcases and disappeared quickly into the crowd moving towards the baggage claim area and airport parking lot.

The passengers from Flight 985 gradually moved on. The crowd waiting for the flight had disappeared from the waiting area. The next groups of passengers from Tokyo, Frankfurt, and Paris started popping out at the same arrival gate. After thirty minutes more of waiting, there was no sign of Dad. Fifty minutes had passed; Dad still did not show up.

"Could he have gotten lost?" I looked at Terry and asked anxiously.

"Is he still being questioned at the airport's Immigration Office?" said Terry, now becoming more concerned.

"Where is Grandpa?" Celine asked.

"Maybe, he got lost. We have to look for him. Terry would you please walk around and see if you can find him? Celine and I will stay here just in case Dad shows up at the arrival gate," I said, reaching for Celine's hand.

"I hope Grandpa doesn't get lost, Mommy," Celine intoned innocently as Terry brushed his way through a moving crowd in hopes of finding Dad.

The San Francisco international terminal in arranged in a circle. If you go around one way, eventually you come back to the same spot where you started. Terry kept walking straight forward and gazing around in all directions but came back to us without sighting Dad in the crowd. "What is going on with Dad? Should we ask the airport to make an announcement for us?" I asked Terry. The airport must provide a lost and found service including help finding people. It was not unusual to broadcast someone's name at the airport. Maybe we should try that, I thought. Terry had another idea. "I wonder if there's another exit?" he said. Sure enough, after asking we discovered that around the back of the main exit there was another exit for passengers changing planes. To get to the exit, we had to go one floor down, walk down a corridor, then go one floor up. When we arrived at this back door, we asked the attendant if he had seen someone of Dad's description. To our relief he had, but indicated that the person had just walked away. Just as I was trying to decide what to do next, I saw an elderly man of short stature and roundish shape pulling a suitcase with one hand and walking briskly towards us. As he came closer, I realized that the elderly man was Dad. He was sweating and out of breath. When he saw us, his face lit up with a huge relief. My heart was racing as our eyes met. I recovered from my emotional distress and instantly felt a heavy stone falling off my shoulders. We all were overwhelmed with joy; we had finally found each other.

Dad looked healthy, but a little pudgy. His remaining hair, all grey, was combed back as always. His facial lines had deepened and wrinkles around his eyes seemed to have doubled since the last time I saw him in Beijing more than two years ago. Dad took a short, deep breath and said in Chinese, "Oh, it took me a long time to find you!" We each took a turn hugging Dad. He responded to our affection politely and awkwardly. Hugging people is not a Chinese custom, at least it wasn't a tradition in mainland China when I lived there. People greet by shaking hands with each other, alternatively by nodding heads.

"Grandpa," Celine said softly and timidly in English.

"You are a big girl now!" Dad responded with a huge smile in Chinese, revealing his cracked, yellow teeth with spaces in between.

Without a verbal reaction, Celine's little pink face lightened up with a grin, as if she understood what her grandpa had just said to her. Last time Dad had seen Celine, she was only six months old. We had stayed with my parents in Beijing for about six months in summer of 1996. I knew, at that time it was the only chance that Celine would have to be with her grandma. During our entire visit, Celine was mostly sleeping, crawling, crying, and peeing on her grandma's bed.

"Did the Immigration Office give you a hard time? Did you get your Green Card?" I asked Dad eagerly.

"Oh, no. The immigration process went surprisingly smoothly," Dad answered. "After getting my documents and Green Card, I didn't know where to go next," Dad went on. "I followed a crowd of people hoping they would lead me to the right exit, but once I was outside, I didn't see you waiting. I became very panicky. I don't speak a word of English. How could I find you?" Dad said.

"Why didn't you ask? You could find someone who spoke Chinese. You know, there are lots of Chinese in San Francisco," I said.

"I don't understand the language and can't read. It's hard to find anyone working at the airport who can speak Mandarin well; most of them speak Cantonese. I must be getting old and losing my mind," Dad sighed.

The first time Dad visited America, he was with Mom. It was in October 1991. Dad was Mom's knight in shining armor during the entire trip from Beijing to San Francisco. They had to stop at the Tokyo Narita International Airport (NRT), then change planes before reaching San Francisco. Mom needed a wheelchair. Dad guided her, took care of her, and ordered special, diabetic meals for Mom on the plane during the trip. With the assistance of airline staff at the three airports, there was no confusion or problems. Mom and Dad didn't get lost. The trip was a big deal for my parents, who had never been out of China and had never under taken such a complicated adventure in their lives. Later on, whenever Dad told the story about the trip, he was always animated. He wanted people to know that he had bravely faced challenges in the foreign countries and that he was smart, alert, and helpful. Dad was Mom's road hero.

This time Dad was traveling on his own, without Mom. To him, getting lost for over an hour at the airport was a traumatic and embarrassing experience. To me, something about him seemed to be significantly different. Dad seemed to be less sure and less confident compared with his first trip to America. Not knowing the language in a strange place, one definitely feels overwhelmed. I certainly can relate to his feeling getting lost at a foreign airport. How can I ever forget about the day when I first landed at the San Francisco airport? I came to the United States as an international student in 1981. I had never left, nor had I been on a plane. I was not aware of any commercial airplane services that were provided to ordinary Chinese citizens in my youth. If flights existed, few could afford them. At that time, only domestic travel was allowed; few people ventured abroad from China. Permission to travel overseas normally was not granted for most, unless you were sent to work at a Chinese embassy as a diplomat or you were selected among the few government delegates who had privilege and were authorized to represent China at world conferences or high level meetings among foreign leaders. Within the country, everything was owned by the government, including its transportation system. Except for bicycles, only public buses and trains were accessible to the masses.

After Nixon visited China in 1971, the doors of both countries opened up to each other. Isolated from the outside world for centuries, the Chinese government had begun to seek friendly relations with Western societies under the leadership of Deng Xiaoping, a reformer and the supreme leader of the People's Republic of China from 1978 to the early 1990s. The outcome of this historical event had encouraged a lot of young Chinese to explore the unknown and entertain the seemingly impossible dream of improving their lives outside China. As a result, learning the English language suddenly became important and trendy. Many people started taking English lessons during their spare time.

Deng came into power in the early 1970s, ending the Chinese Cultural Revolution that started in 1966. The Chinese Cultural Revolution was violent and resulted in nationwide social and political chaos, and economic upheaval. After many years of being shutdown during the Cultural Revolution, universities had opened their doors once again. I was one of the lucky ones who took the opportunity and went on to finish my college degree and, later on, to teach in a well-known institute in Beijing. By the late 1970s I was restless, eager to see the world, and hungry for freedom. I wanted to improve my English language skills in an English-speaking country with the hope of becoming a better teacher when I returned.

No one had believed I would be able to travel abroad to study in America; even I thought the possibility was a long shot. After more than two years of trying and dealing with the local officials, I finally got permission from the government and later obtained a student visa issued by the American Embassy in Beijing. I was in my late twenties and determined to leave for a better education in America. The night before my departure, I put two hundred U.S. dollars, my entire fortune, in a small cotton bag, and then sewed it inside my underwear. The next morning I was eager to start my adventure. There was a long good-bye at the Beijing airport. After all, in my entire family no one had ever laid foot on foreign soil before, not even among the friends that I knew. I managed to put on a fake smile because I didn't want my parents to detect any uncertainties from my facial and body language that could lead them to believe that I was unsure about my journey ahead. At the departure gate, Mom and Dad both took each of my hands and held them tightly for a long time, as if they were about to let their precious gem slip through their fingers. Once it was gone, it could never be traced again. Finally they let my hands go.

"Write us a letter soon once you get there." Dad said.

"I will," I muttered while holding my tears in my eyes.

"We are still young in our early fifties. Once we have reached sixty years of age, we wish you will be back from America to stay for good," said Mom.

"Em..." I didn't know what to say and nodded my head instead.

"Take good care of yourself there," Dad added.

"I will."

I turned my back on their misty eyes and walked away without looking back.

Soon I was sitting on the plane, suddenly starting to doubt my adventure ahead. I was afraid! I had planned for this moment for over two years. I was desperate to leave, yet had never truly thought about what lay ahead on my new journey. The truth was I didn't really know anyone in America except for a long-distant relative who was in Nebraska at the time. I had never met my so-called relative before. He had agreed to be my sponsor on paper as long as I was applying to pursue my studies at a university in the United States.

I was now sitting on a plane feeling cold and sick. I took out an airline paper bag from the seat pocket in front of me and threw up. In preparing for the next wave of vomit, I asked the persons on either side of me permission to use their paper bags. I was miserable. It seemed to me that I was heading into oblivion. My final destiny was Omaha, Nebraska. I had to transfer at the San Francisco airport, my first U.S. stop. When the plane landed at the airport, before getting off I held my breath and told myself to be calm and ready to face the fear of the unknown.

Red, blue, and green lights seemed to be flashing constantly at the international terminal. The sound of bustle and chatter from people bombarded at me from all directions and the smell of the airport made me feel dizzy and light-headed. I felt as if I was in outer space. I had majored in English in college and taught English as a second language in Beijing and thought I would have no problem understanding Americans. I was wrong. As soon as I stepped out into the terminal, I found out quickly the locals talked way too fast. I had no idea what to do and where to go at the arrival gate. I panicked when I heard an announcement that my flight from San Francisco to Omaha had been cancelled due to an airline strike. Disbelieving my own hearing, I double-checked it with several fellow passengers from the same plane. It was confirmed. I didn't know anyone here, nor did I know where to stay in San Francisco. However, I knew there was no turning back. I didn't even have enough money to buy a return ticket. All I had was two hundred dollars hiding inside my underwear. That was it, not a penny more. I was preoccupied with my thoughts, waiting for another shoe to drop, not far from the arrival gate, when I heard a voice, a familiar, Chinese voice. "Do you need any help?" a seemingly trustworthy young man with a friendly smile asked me. He seemed to be in his early thirties, was wearing a light brown cotton shirt and blue jeans, and held a cardboard sign that said, 'Welcome to San Francisco. Greetings from the Chinese San Francisco Consul.' I desperately explained to him about my unsettling situation. "You could stay at the Chinese Consulate and catch a flight to Omaha tomorrow," he made me an offer that I could not resist. This young man, who I had never met before, was my salvation. I was rescued by the Chinese San Francisco Consul. It turned out later that I had to stay at the consulate for several days and did not get on another plane until the airline strike was finally over. The memory of my similar experience reminded me that once I had been in Dad's shoes. I could empathize with his frustrations of being lost. After all, I had been there.

Dad didn't seem to be so confident this time around. Underneath his smile I sensed sadness and loneliness. Mom had passed away in 2001. Even though her passing had been anticipated after her years of battling diabetes, Dad had never been truly prepared for her death and was crushed by it. I suppose that no matter how hard one prepares for it, death is always difficult to handle. Dad was extremely sad and seemed unable to cope with his loss. After all, Mom and Dad had been together for more than fifty years. Dad didn't want to leave the house or travel after Mom's passing. Finally I was able to persuade him to apply for a visa and join me in America. After two years of waiting, Dad was here with me today. He could rebuild his life again in America, I hoped. This time he was here as a new immigrant, not as a foreign visitor, with his permanent visa, a Green Card.

America had been a land of opportunity for many people before and would be for him as well. The opportunity for him to live with me in America meant a new beginning. Dad and I had always bonded well in my youth. The bond was now strained because we had been apart from each other for so many years. Dad and I could re-establish our relationship with shared feelings, interests, and experiences. Dad would have an opportunity to age in comfort and to build a closer relationship with his American granddaughter, who was first introduced to him in Beijing when she was six months old. He had followed her growth and development from a long distance through the frames of photos that we had sent him over the years. Dad could live in style, enjoy the rest of his life, and reside permanently on American soil.

As Terry drove us back to our coastal mountain home, we passed a chain of small cities, rolling hills covered with grasses turning green after the recent spring rains, half-filled reservoirs, and coastal mountains where redwoods stood tall. Dad remained quiet in the car. I wondered if he needed a moment of peace after such a long journey, or if he wished to take a rest after his mix-up at the airport. Perhaps he was thinking about Mom, about their first American trip together twelve years ago. Or perhaps he was quietly anticipating what lay ahead. I was also lost in my thoughts on the way home. My situation was much different than when I first landed in America. I was now a citizen, a homeowner, and had a steady job. My home was now Dad's. He would eventually learn to like his new home. America was a land of opportunity. Would Dad be able to embrace it?

2. Love Had Everything to Do with It

Mom and Dad in Wu Han

Could Dad ultimately find happiness in his new home and be a benefactor of this land of freedom? Could he embrace it with open arms, especially this time when he was here without Mom? Twelve years ago, during their trip to America, Mom was his constant comfort and emotional help when Dad was in distress; she also supplied her support and encouragement to Dad when needed. Their relationship was built on the basis of equal terms and mutual respect. Their bond was not only physical, but also emotional. Mom was the love of his life and his anchor.

I always wonder if one can truly love another human being unconditionally and unselfishly. Are the fates of Romeo and Juliet, or Bella and Edward, merely literary fantasies on paper? As I think about my parents' journey through life together, I begin believing in the existence of such a wonder. Beyond any doubt, the sense of admiration between Dad and Mom was indescribable. Devotion is the word that sums up their love story. The love between them was not dramatic and short-lived like a fireworks display, but one of enduring permanence, like the predictable bloom of flowers in spring. One of my all-time favorite songs is Tina Turner's "What's love got to do with it." The lyrics downplay the significance of love, relegating this to a phantom emotion emanating mostly from physical attraction. This, however, is in sharp contrast to the old-fashioned love that characterizes the love between Mom and Dad. I don't suggest that there was no physical attraction between them, but their love for one another was more than that. It was logical, respectable, and profound in a sweet old-fashioned way that is rarely seen in the material world where people often confuse money with self-worth.

Shortly after being introduced by their colleagues in Wu Han, one of China's most important transportation hubs south of the Yungzi River, my parents combined their blankets, sheets, suitcases, and a few simple pieces of furniture, and moved into a one-room unit. They then got married. They were twenty-one, an age too young to rent a car from major American car-rental companies and just past the legal drinking age in the United States. Back then Dad was skinny and his trim waistline earned him the nickname Chopsticks. Dad was quiet, calm, and good natured. He was always eager to learn new things, but seldom followed his new ideas through once he started. One time, out of the blue, Dad wanted to learn how to play the Chinese flute, but quit after only a few lessons. I still tease him about it whenever I get a chance. Conversely, Mom was outgoing, energetic, and determined. She was interested in so many things in life. She would try something new and stick with it. Table tennis (ping pong) was a very popular sport in China during the 60s and the 70s. Mom enjoyed the sport and loved the competition. She participated in many ping pong meets whenever she could find time during the weekends. In the 70s people in China normally went to work on Sundays and only had Saturdays off during the weekends. On Saturdays my parents barely had enough time to finish the house chores or run errands. Mom somehow managed to find time to perfect her offensive and defensive ping pong strokes. "I will take care of the house cleaning. I will get the groceries after that," Dad often said to Mom. Mom would nod her head with a big smile before leaving for her practice. If there were no ping pong meets on either Friday nights or Saturdays, Mom would take me with her to her ping pong practices. Her push, chop, and block strokes were precise and forceful. Whenever she had executed a winning smash, or followed through on a powerful forehand or backhand stroke, overwhelmed with joy she would shout aloud with excitement, "Yes. Yes!" Mom was very competitive and became a quite good ping pong player. Dad always supported her wholeheartedly. Whenever Mom won her competitions, Dad said to her proudly, "Well done... well done. Good job!" Dad and Mom shared many common interests in their lives, yet had different approaches to learning new things. The outcome of their individual approach in learning often produced different results. However, their relationship was based on mutual understanding that enriched their admiration for each other and a dynamic that made their union work. That is an attraction of opposites, I suppose.

On the surface, from her friends' and colleagues' points of view, Mom seemed to be energetic and healthy. In reality, Mom's health was gradually declining. By the mid-1980s, due to a lack of treatment, her type-one diabetes had worsened. Medical professionals call type-one diabetes, "insulin-dependent diabetes". Insulin allows the body cells to absorb and metabolize glucose. Without insulin, glucose remains in the blood stream and the cells don't have access to the energy they need. As a result, the body lacks energy and the high levels of glucose in the blood can damage the blood vessels and organs they come in contact with. For a long time Mom had refused to use insulin. She made excuses. "It is not good to use it every day. I will have to depend on it. The shots will make me gain weight." Later on, if I questioned her on the phone from the States about not using insulin, Mom would say that she couldn't use it because there wasn't enough insulin supply in China. I wondered if that was the case, or if it was just another excuse. Insulin was first invented in China, according to my parents, who had a tendency to declare that China was the birthplace for many famous and important inventions. If so, how could China, the home country of the invention, not have enough insulin supplies for its people, I wondered? Later I found out that Fredrick G. Banting and Charles H. Best, two Canadians, actually received the Nobel Prize in 1923 for discovering insulin. I have no idea who was the first to produce insulin for large-scale use in the world. My recent research suggests that after "the determination of the primary structure of insulin" by British biochemist Frederick Sanger, also recipient of the 1958 Nobel Prize in chemistry, China succeeded in the chemical synthesis of insulin in 1965. However, the Cultural Revolution interfered with the research process, resulting in a delay in the publication of final resolution of this study until 1971.

It would appear that insulin was definitely not discovered in China, however the question of whether or not China was the first country to produce insulin in large quantities is unclear. My research suggests that China has produced insulin from animal tissue since 1981 and insulin originating from human tissue since 2005, mostly at Wanbang Biopharma Co., one of the country's biggest insulin manufactures in Xuzhou, a city in Jiangsu Province in southern China. Supplies of insulin were either lacking or too expensive before that time and were perhaps also delayed by the chaos of the Cultural Revolution. Even though Mom's reason for not using insulin seemed to be based on her own beliefs rather than limitations in terms of supply, the dates of mass production of either animal or human insulin were in any case too late to be of use to Mom.

Mom was once found lying unconscious on a neighborhood street. Her body was covered with bruises and she had black eyes on her swollen face. After she had a series of falls caused by fainting over the course a few months, she realized that she could not function normally at her job any more due to her illness and subsequently had to retire early. She retired in her mid-fifties. The decision was extremely hard on Mom, who was known as a workaholic. Her type-one diabetes had affected her weight, vision, legs, and heart. Stubbornly she continued to refuse to have any insulin shots that were needed to move her blood sugar into cells, where it could be stored and later used for energy. In type-one diabetes, cells in the pancreas produce little or no insulin. As a result, Mom was in constant pain, feeling tired, and plagued with low energy. She was short tempered and often hard to please. Soon after her retirement, her health took a nose dive. By the early 1990s, Mom went totally blind as a result of her untreated diabetes.

While parents of my childhood friends would save half of their earnings and splurge on a bike or a sewing machine, which was considered to be trendy at a time, my folks would spend most of their monthly income on efforts to satisfy their palates. Mom loved to eat and especially loved gourmet food. Who wouldn't? But her degree of loving food, to me, was beyond the norm. "It is all about taste," she once said. Mom was extremely picky about how her meal should be prepared. "There is an art in cooking," said she. "Good taste depends on your cooking skills. When cooking, you must know what ingredients to use, how high or low the temperature should be, and precisely how long it takes." She would not allow Dad and me to go near the stove while she was cooking. Before she lost her vision, she did all our cooking. Dad and I were usually relegated to the second rank as her assistants. Our job was to wash vegetables, pots and pans, or occasionally cut vegetables with detailed instructions from Mom. Dad wasn't qualified to be a meat cutter. Mom didn't trust his cutting skills. She wanted her meat to be cut in certain sizes and distinct shapes. One of her favorite dishes was stir-fried cilantro with diced pork. The Chinese cilantro (also called coriander or Chinese parsley) that was used as the main green in stir-fry at my home had large, fresh leaves and long stems with a strong aromatic flavor. Mom's hands and brain were the instruments of measurement. She made up her own recipe as she cooked. Using a wok, her stir-fried cilantro and pork typically contained:

Cooking oil (Any amount and any kind you wish. The cooking oil available to us at that time was corn or peanut.)

- Salt (Any kind)

- Pepper (Either black or white)

- Lots of fresh, long-stem cilantro (Cut into 2-inch long pieces. This is the main portion of the dish.)

- Diced pork (Any amount you wish. Cut into 1-inch long pieces. Marinated with salt, cooking wine, back or white pepper and soy sauce for a few minutes before cooking.)

- A few slices of green onions

- A few slices of ginger

- A few slices of garlic

Method: Stir fry salt, pepper, green onions, ginger and garlic first, then add diced pork, and later cilantro. (Prep: 30 min. Cook: 3 to 5 min.)

Being a typical "Yes Man," Dad was a happy assistant and eager to please Mom. When Mom wanted beef for supper, Dad made sure not to buy pork. When Mom wanted chicken for lunch, Dad made sure that he didn't purchase lamb instead. He didn't want to change the course, even if he had wished to do so. He always delivered the raw materials for meals on wheels – his bicycle, that is. Dad was a vegetarian who wouldn't touch any meat products, but he would go all-out for Mom's craving for animal protein. In the 70s and 80s, supplies of food and goods were low in stores in Beijing. Often Dad had to shop in several different grocery stores in order to get what Mom wished. Dad's major form of transportation was a bike. He would pedal it in snow or ride it rain or shine. Not a single complaint was heard from Dad who was always willing to do anything for Mom.

Like other couples, there were ups and downs in their relationship. They argued about silly insignificant things sometimes, but their fights normally didn't last long. A few hours after their argument was over, Dad would start making the first move by wise cracking. The tension between Mom and Dad loosened up immediately and Mom's face soon cracked into a smile again. Cracking jokes with each other was their medicine and therapy in coping with the difficulties surrounding Mom's long-term illness. Joking about themselves was also their way to show their affection and devotion to each other. They enjoyed each other's company tremendously and entertained themselves throughout their most challenging times, including the Cultural Revolution.

Though both of them were born in the Year of Horse, one of the twelve animals which appear in the Chinese zodiac, Mom was the Dragon Lady, while Dad was a bowl of noodle soup – a gentle man with a soft and easy touch. Horse people display, as *Chinese Zodiac: Your guide to Chinese Astrology* points out, such character traits as "strength, energy, and an outgoing nature. Extremely animated, horses thrive when they're the center of attention. Always in search of a good time, horses keep the crowds happy with their humor and their wit." They are normally compatible with a Dog or Tiger. If Horses marry to each other, one of them had better "hide their egoism." Being with Mom, Dad certainly learned how to hide his ego.

The situation in the household reversed after Mom's health went increasingly downhill. Dad had to retire and become her caregiver. Although it was too late to prevent the deterioration of her health, Mom finally agreed to use insulin. Dad gave her insulin shots three times a day and also became the chief chef because Mom didn't trust anyone to do the job but him. Mom micro-managed him to death, especially while Dad was cooking. "Add a little bit soy sauce…add some black pepper. Okay, it is done," Mom directed. Even though she could not see, Mom still instructed Dad when he was stir-fry cooking, their most common mode of preparing supper. She gave endless directions to Dad and would only let up after she was completely satisfied. Several times Dad hired someone to help with the cooking, but after a few try-outs, he had to let the person go because Mom wasn't pleased with the taste of the meal she had prepared. In comparison, Dad was by far the best pitcher in the league.

By the end of the 90s, Mom was restricted to a wheelchair and was totally dependent on Dad. Dad was the one who pushed her around and took her to all her hospital visits. A few times in the middle of the night, Dad had to rush Mom to the urgent care facility nearby. Towards the end of her life Mom had to remain in the hospital in order to get medicine and proper care. Needless to say, she didn't like the hospital food. Dad's routine during this period consisted entirely of preparing and bringing Mom breakfast, lunch, and dinner, three times a day. He faithfully did this for eighteen years until Mom passed away.

Nursing homes were unpopular in China in the past and continue to suffer a negative image. People just did not believe that a nursing home was the best solution for the elderly or the disabled. Someone who would send his or her loved ones to a place like that was often judged as an immoral person by friends and family members. The emotional toll of being Mom's caregiver on a daily basis was stressful and traumatic for Dad. Once while I was in Beijing for a visit, Dad explained to me in tears why he couldn't travel anywhere like other people did. "I can't even take a day trip to the city park. I am worried about your mom. She needs shots three times a day. Who will do it? Who will cook for her if I am not home? When my friends go for vacations, I stay behind. I can't take the time off and go with them," Dad went on. I looked at Dad feeling helpless. Yes, Dad could hire an assistant, I thought. There were plenty of young girls from the poor countryside who had flooded into Beijing looking for jobs in recent years. They were desperate to be hired as an in-home caregiver or a housekeeper. Most households in Dad's neighborhood had hired maids from the provinces, reflecting a recent trend in the city.

Dad had to put his self interest on hold and put up with the consequences and Mom's demands. He gradually learned to accept the reality and made the best of it. He even learned to enjoy life a little. "I'm sorry that because of me you can't do the things that you want," Mom said to Dad, her voice cracking. "I'm fine. I don't want to go anywhere," Dad tried to comfort her. He then would make a joke of their situation; Mom started smiling again. Somehow, for more than eighteen years, Dad had managed to survive his daily tasks and all the accompanying restrictions on his life.

I am always amazed by my parents' affection and devotion to each other, and touched by the tender care given by Dad to Mom. How could one be so unselfish and sacrificing to another being? This person would have to be a super being. I imagine those eighteen years would be a long hardship for anyone, especially for the one who had to provide constant care to a disabled person. Could I have given that kind of devotion if I were in Dad's shoes? Could I have provided that kind of focus and endurance? I'm not sure. Could I say to myself constantly that another person was more important than me? I frequently doubt if I could truly be such a super hero. The meaning of the word "love" seems to be so simple, yet so deep and mysteriously profound that it is beyond my ability to define. Perhaps William Shakespeare, Stephanie Meyer, and Tina Turner have already defined love for me in their love songs and stories. Nevertheless, I am overwhelmed by this profound human emotion that seems to be so concrete, yet so hard to focus in my imagination. What I do know in my heart is that the love between Dad and Mom was more like a song in the deepest sea than waves on the surface of a pond.

A few days before Mom passed away, she said to Dad that she knew her time was coming. "You should find someone after this is over," Mom told Dad. "Who would want me? I am too old to find anyone," Dad answered jokingly and thoughtfully. That was his typical tone; it was a method to disguise his pain if he had to face a tough circumstance. Once I suggested, "Dad, why don't you find someone that you can share your life with? I know she can never replace Mom, but you need to enjoy your life, too." I went on, "By the way, this person has to treat you well and care for your health." Dad thought about it for a few seconds, then answered me simply, "I like being by myself." He went on to say that he felt content and would like to remain single for the rest of his life. Dad had already found the love of his life. That was Mom. No one could ever take her place. It's not my position to judge anyone who would decide a different life path if in the same situation as my parents. The devotion that I witnessed between Mom and Dad was pure; indeed, love had everything to do with it.

By the time I woke from my deep thoughts about Dad and Mom, our car had already passed the coastal mountain summit and the clouds in the sky had turned heavy gray. We were only a few minutes away from our destination.

3. One Hundred Steps

When we finally arrived at home from the airport, it was supper time and already dark outside. I promised Dad a tour of our garden the next morning and quickly led him to his room while Terry was bringing in his suitcases. We had converted one of our bedrooms into a built-in home office a couple of years ago. In preparation for Dad's arrival, we set up a single bed in the office and turned it back into a bedroom for Dad. The room is radiant in the afternoons with bright sunlight descending through a large skylight. Lying on the bed, one can see the canopy of a tall redwood tree taking a huge bite out of blue roof of the sky. At night the moon and stars sparkle through the redwood that branches out into the indistinct sky. Dad's bed was loaded with a down comforter and new cover, pillows, and a new set of bed sheets. The room was also equipped with a new 19" inch flat LCD TV bought at the local electronics store. Dad is a news junky and accordingly loves watching TV. He can watch the same TV news program again and again without getting bored. Old news becomes new news; new news gets Dad excited. He recycles the news and enjoys the reruns. People can get high by doing weird things; Dad certainly can get hyper by watching the same old news.

To match the TV set and the room color, we moved a black massage chair that I purchased online into the bedroom. I have fallen into the trend of buying things online, for better or worse. On the Internet, the photo of this chair looked attractive and well-made. Once it was shipped to the house, the real product did not seem to live up to what I had imagined. This purchase was my last online shopping foray for furniture, I decided. Call me old fashioned, but I still prefer the traditional hands-on buying experience in a real store. I feel safe, secure, and good about my final choice if I can touch and see a product real-time before buying it. In this case, the chair was made from fake leather and didn't turn out to be the top to bottom quality product I hoped for. It did shake and vibrate, but didn't really massage very well. Nevertheless, after using it for ten minutes with the chair's own heater, it magically made you feel comfortable and sleepy; you didn't wish to get up again for a long time.

In northern California the climate is mild all year around, although decidedly cooler and wetter in winter. Inside our house it's never warm enough according to Dad's standard, even though it has a central heating system. He is always afraid of cold temperatures, therefore I also added a small electrical heater to his bedroom setup. We don't have the same kind of weather as Beijing. We don't heat the houses like people do there either. Terry and I usually keep the room temperature somewhere around 68 Fahrenheit in the winter. In Beijing, the heating system in the neighborhood where Dad lives is centrally controlled by an ancient system of piping hot water to heat homes through radiators. The system normally begins working on the first day of November and ends on the last day of March. Inside it is hot and steaming like a kettle, while outside it is freezing cold and dry. Sometimes the outside temperature is ten below zero. So much water and energy are wasted on human beings during such a long period. I have no idea if afterwards they make any efforts to recycle the heating water to save the energy that is used to keep people feeling comfortable. It seems that if humans want anything, then humans get it. Dad prefers a hot environment and being toasted inside. During their visit here in 1991, my parents complained about being cold all the time, even when the electric heating and the fireplace were running nonstop in the house. This time it would be better, I thought. Dad had his own electrical heater that should keep him warm. If he closed his bedroom door and turned it on, he would be toasty and satisfied.

I suggested Dad take a hot shower to make him feel relaxed after such a long flight. "I will prepare noodle soup for supper. It will be ready soon after your shower," I said to Dad. He thought about it for a few seconds, then took my advice. My persuasion worked. Dad doesn't like to take a shower, nor does he like the water in swimming pools. He is a dry duck. "I had a bad experience with water and almost drowned in the river I was crossing," he once told me. Most households did not have showers in bathrooms when I grew up. In my neighborhood there was a central bath house divided into separate sections for men and women. If you wanted to take a shower or a bath, you would pay three yuan for using the facility each time. I only took a shower once or twice a month in the bath house. The rest of time I washed my feet using a bucket of water and changed my underclothes every night before going to bed. It's hard to imagine how I did it then. Nowadays I can't even go to sleep without taking a shower at night. It's sort of like Darwin's evolution theory, I suppose. "Over the course of time, organisms adapt with varying degrees of success to changes in habitats ... the surviving species of a given period are the ones best suited to the environment." Back then, most people that I knew didn't even take a shower every month. Dad was one of them. "Taking too many showers is not good for your skin. You will lose the natural oil that protects your skin," he said both seriously and jokingly. Dad would go to the bath house once every couple of months. If Mom forgot to remind him, he would never go. The conversations about Dad taking a shower would normally go like this:

Mom: "You are so dirty. Go to take a shower today."

Dad: "How about tomorrow? I am busy today."

Mom: "No. Today!"

Dad: "Okay, okay. I will go tonight."

Dad gave in at the end. Not until the recent decade did most Chinese homes have a shower or a bath facility. Even to this date, Dad takes a shower only once in a week; once a day only if it is hot in summer. Dad doesn't like to play with water nor does he wish to dive into a pool, a river, or a lake. Swimming is not Dad's cup of tea. He doesn't want to have anything to do with water, except for drinking it. On the contrary, I swim five or six times a week. Swimming is more than an exercise for me. It is a therapy or an antidote that keeps me calm, relaxed, and grounded mentally. I am neither fish nor fowl; I am neither a fast nor a slow swimmer. I am neutral in terms of speed. I am not competitive in the water. This doesn't mean I don't have a competitive nature. In general my philosophy is to compete with myself to set personal goals. There is a swimming pool at the local health club that I belong to. I use it five times a week. People on each side of my lane, often zip by me with laser speed. They look like fish searching for food back and forth in the water. They are the go-getters in grand style. Every stroke and each lap seem to mean something special to them. Their talents lie behind their showcased free style, breast stroke, backstroke, and butterfly. They seem to be able to do any style they want. I, on the other hand, am a mediocre swimmer, and can only do one style, breast stroke. My daughter once confronted me, "Mom, what you are doing is not really breast stroke." In the eyes of my daughter, I was not a stroking star. To my mind, I am not there to compete. I have my own style, my own pace. Swimming is a therapy that is good for my mind and soul. If tired or frustrated, I immediately feel reborn after swimming. It keeps a balance of my brain, my health, and my work, and enables me to cope with challenges in life.

Soon after Dad joined us, I once encouraged him to go to the pool at our health club with Celine and me.

"Why don't you swim with us today?"

"I don't know how."

"Celine could teach you. The pool water is shallow."

"I'll try when the weather gets warmer."

"It's quite hot today."

"I'll think about it."

He had thought about it for a long time and had never given me an answer, but finally he gave in. On a warm day he carefully descended into the pool, guided by a handrail and Celine's encouragement from down in the pool, with me looking on from further away. He never got further than the bottom of the steps. After about five minutes in waist deep water, still glued to the handrail, he retreated to the hot tub.

"What happened Dad?" I asked when I had finished my laps.

"That water is too cold," he responded with an exaggerated shiver.

That was the end of his swimming foray.

After a shower Dad was energetic and refreshed, but he was still wearing the same drab outfit from China, which included a dark grey shirt. On top of it was a black wool sweater and on top of that, a light grey wool vest. He had on a pair of dark grey pants made of 62 percent polyester, 34 percent rayon, and 4 percent spandex. Beneath the pants there was a pair of 100 percent cotton long underwear. Dad would never wish to go without his long underwear even during late spring and early summer. He wanted to keep his legs warm all the time. He would eventually give in and wear one pair of pants if the temperature rose to 85°F degrees or above. I bought Dad several new shirts, sweaters, and pants, but he put them away and saved them for China. "People in China now are wearing fancy clothes. It is casual here," said Dad. While staying with us, he changed his outfit once a month. If switching, he rotated it with only one set of clothes. The colors of his outerwear were kept simple: blue, grey, or black.

Noodle soup was served often at home in my youth. My choice of having noodles for supper proved to be an excellent idea that was obviously confirmed at the dinner table. Dad enjoyed it immensely after his long flight, followed by a few cups of green tea. I finally felt relaxed enough to put my feet up. Under the kitchen lights, I examined Dad's profile closely. He had noticeably aged. Skin winkles evolve over the travel of time and his birthmark was still positioned in the middle of his chin. His facial skin over the years had deviated from that of his youth with deepened lines and scars. Dad is not a tall man. As a child, to me he seemed to be taller than his actual height. I had always pictured him that way. This time around, he looked even shorter. If we stood close together, Dad and I seemed to be the same height. It reminded me of the old saying, "the older you become, the shorter you get." Dad must have shrunk.

Traveling through several time zones by plane can make anyone feel tired. If it is 8:30 PM in Northern California, then it is 11:30 AM in Beijing. Whenever I visit China, the journey there seems to be easier than returning in terms of adjusting to the local time. I find it difficult to make the switch after coming back to the States. My body is telling me to go in one direction while my brain is directing me to go in the opposite direction. After returning on a flight from China, I cannot fall asleep at night. But by the crack of dawn, I am totally exhausted and do not wish to get up. This pattern usually repeats for four or five days. To no one's surprise, the new time zone had disrupted Dad's sleep-wake cycle and it took him more than a week to shed his jet lag.

While Dad was with us, Celine was away at school; and Terry and I were at work during the daytime. I subscribed to a Chinese newspaper and made sure Dad could watch a Chinese TV channel from San Francisco so that he wouldn't feel left out or isolated. It was time for him to settle into his new home. I suggested that Dad should start learning English and practice it on us when we came home.

"Yes. I have a tape-recorder. I can listen to the English lessons on the tape I bought in China before I left," agreed Dad.

"At least you should know some common phrases like, how are you? I am hungry, or where is the bathroom?" I suggested.

"How do you say 'big belly' in Chinese?" Celine joined the conversation, noticing the fat cellulose on her grandpa's midsection, then giggled. I translated her question to Dad.

"Nutty girl," Dad said in Chinese to Celine with a huge grin.

"Celine, why don't you teach Grandpa two words in English and Grandpa teach you two words in Chinese every day?" I went on.

"Uhhh…"

There was a long pause. The conversation went dead afterwards. I knew I had just touched a subject of a commitment that to follow one had to have persistence or a strong will. I wasn't quite sure either of them had these requirements. The bottom line I wished for was that Dad would be able to communicate with Celine and the locals at a basic level of English. Hopefully he could also find something interesting to do and live in a meaningful life while he was in America.

Right after Mom passed away, Dad started having high blood pressure. For most people with high blood pressure, the exact cause is unknown. With a family history of low blood pressure, it is hard to imagine how Dad could have any issues. Perhaps the stress of losing Mom after years of marriage was the key factor that had triggered his high blood pressure. Our mountain home sits on a peaceful hillside blanketed with a misty coastal redwood forest. It is on the south side of the hill that blocks the highway traffic noises emanating from the northern direction. In the early hours or later afternoon you can hear birds singing and often catch sight of deer jogging through the neighborhood woods. Some neighbors have even spotted wild turkeys, bobcats, coyotes, and the occasional signs of a mountain lion wandering down the road. I believe it is a perfect environment for someone who needs relaxation and peaceful meditation. That someone was Dad. In addition, his heavy stature had signaled a warning sign about his health; his blood pressure could be getting worse due to the absence of exercise. Health and physical fitness are closely related. If swimming didn't belong in Dad's fitness routine, what did belong? Walking! I must get him moving and walking around, I thought. One night about two weeks after he had arrived, I said to Dad,

"Don't sit in the house all day along. Take a walk or help to water the plants in the garden. It is good for your health."

Speaking of the plants, the luscious garden that Terry took great pride in was presented to Dad one day after he had arrived. Terry and I had painstakingly revegetated the entire one-acre property ourselves. We had pulled the weeds, cut back the overgrown shrubs, replaced dead perennials on the ground or in the pots, planted new fruit trees, and felt overjoyed with the results of our labors each year. A few pots of flowers outdoors needed to be watered by using the garden hose every day. Dad was eager to take on the task, unfortunately he wasn't used to using high water pressure through a nozzle and succeeded in blasting the soil away from the roots of the now hydroponic plants. Fortunately for the plants, he lost interest after only a few days.

"Your brother thinks I can live until eighty years old," Dad replied without giving me a "yes" or "no" answer to my suggestion of walking or my request for his continued support of those outdoor potted flowers.

Most of my family friends consider eighty as a magic number: the atomic number in chemistry and physics, and a semi-perfect number in number theory. If you can live to be eighty years of age, you have reached a significant monument. Eighty is hailed as a milestone in one's life's work. Eighty was the perfect number Dad aimed for and a goal he looked forward to. Suddenly an old Chinese saying came to my mind as I was having these random thoughts: "To be able to live until ninety-nine years of age, one must walk one hundred steps after each meal." (*Fan hou bai bu zou, neng huo jiu shi jiu*) Trying to raise this bar higher, I reminded Dad about the phrase. "Remember? You could even live to be one hundred." "Oh, yes. A good idea. We should walk," he responded with a smile.

Dad was isolated here in our mountainside small town, especially during the daytime. Although there is a large Chinese population in the Bay Area, there are only handfuls of Chinese that can be occasionally spotted in the town where we live. It's like seeing rare birds on a field trip. There is no one in the neighborhood that I am aware of who can understand Mandarin Chinese besides Terry and I. Once a friendly couple in the neighborhood ran into Dad on the road, greeting him politely by addressing him as "Old Wei," followed by "How are you?" (*Ni hau*) in Chinese. It was the only phrase that they knew and that they had learned from me in advance of Dad's arrival. After their small vocabulary was exhausted, their verbal communication was limited to non-verbal but enthusiastic hand gestures, head nodding, and smiles. Nevertheless, I applauded their efforts. It was up to me to be Dad's savior. I would go for a walk with Dad after supper. Walking together would be a bonding time between a father and a daughter. Besides, walking would help Dad to lose some weight and perhaps get him into a good shape, or so I hoped.

It had been two weeks since Dad had arrived. One night after a bowl of noodle soup, I said to him, "Let's go for a walk." Dad was beaming with smiles and ready to go. "Sure. Let me grab my jacket," he said. "It is already March, and no longer cold outside," I responded to him while I was walking towards the garage door. He caught up with me in the driveway with his grey jacket in hand. Dad was wearing the same outfit that he wore when he got off the plane two weeks earlier; still the same black wool sweater, the same light grey vest and underneath the layers was the same dark grey shirt, and of course, that same pair of dark grey pants. He never tired of those drab grey, black, and blue colors. Once I bought him a pair of boxer shorts. He later complained that the multiple patterns of the boxers were too colorful. As far as artistry is concerned, he is a simple man of one color dimension. Perhaps his taste of color has nothing to do with artistry and more to do with genetics. Dad has color blindness. It is more common for males in a family to inherit this gene. However, in my family I inherited color blindness, rather than my brother. Lucky me! My condition is milder than Dad's. He would feel totally lost in a multi-color demanding situation.

On the other hand, perhaps his color preferences have nothing to do with his being color blind, but are simply a reflection of his education, learning experiences, or the environment where he grew up. It is said that during the ancient days only the emperors and their close relatives could adorn themselves with red and yellow. Yellow corresponds to the center of earth and was reserved for royalty. According to Chinese lore, "the reddish color of earth and yellow are symbolic of the mixture of earth and heaven. Heaven is abstruse and earth ... it unfolds and mingles yin and yang", the two complementary forces in nature and the central principle of the cosmos. Red corresponds to good fortune, joy, and positive energy. These two colors were the symbols of power and authority. Only the Emperor's close family members could have homes with red walls and yellow roof tiles. Lower commoners weren't allowed to paint their houses with red and yellow and could only have blue, grey, black, or white walls and roof tiles. Even to this day, the temples and palaces where the emperors had once stayed are still maintained with their original red and yellow colors. Later on, during the ten years of Cultural Revolution, any colorful objects or even flowers were considered decadent, provocative, and bad. The Red Guards had red banners. Yellow symbolized the sun; according to the Red Guards the bright sunlight was the spirit of Mao Zedong, the revolutionary, political theorist, and leader of the Chinese Communist Party. If you weren't a Red Guard, to be safe you would have to stick with black, grey, and blue. Dad was criticized as being a capitalist. A capitalist could never be a Red Guard. Perhaps this is why Dad is so comfortable with drab colors.

As Dad and I started pacing slowly, I turned to Dad and said,

"One hundred steps after each meal. Let's try to do it everyday, if we can."

"Okay, all right."

"If you eat right, take care of yourself, and walk at least once a day, you will live to be one hundred years of age."

"Oh, I hope so, I hope so."

Our neighborhood sits on the lower part of a dead-end road that runs steeply from north to south. One needs strong leg muscles to walk uphill to the dead-end. On each side of the road grow beautiful redwood trees, native to only coastal California and the southwestern corner of Oregon. Although in prehistoric times redwoods covered vast areas of the globe, they are currently restricted to the West Coast of the United States. There is a small population of a close relative of the California redwood, the dawn redwood, in China, that unlike the species in California, loses its needles in the fall. The redwood here is an evergreen and long-lived. The individuals of this species include the tallest trees on earth and individual specimens can live more than two thousand years. The coastal redwood usually grows in the mountains where there is more precipitation and fog drift from the incoming moisture off the ocean. In addition to the redwood trees, a smattering of tan oak, buckeye, bay, elderberry, pine, Douglas fir, and maple trees also eek out an existence in the shadows of the giant redwoods in our neighborhood.

The coastal fog had lifted by the late morning and began rolling back again in the late afternoon. Although it was summer, it was a cool and misty day. The sun was sinking gradually as Dad and I were slowly walking up the hill. Red shafts of sunlight beamed through the redwoods. The trunks of these tall giants were reaching upward, seeking the light far above the forest floor and the misty shroud below. In such tranquility, Dad seemed to enjoy every step. "I always love trees," Dad said. "I grew up in a small village surrounded by mountains and trees," he took a deep breath and resumed walking. Dad had talked about loving trees before, but it was nice for me to hear it again, especially on this side of the Pacific Ocean. He liked it here, I thought. Dad took another deep breath and said, "My mother, your grandma, passed away when I was about five. After that I had to live with my grandma, your great grandma, and other relatives." He stopped for a moment and said memorably, "I also went with my dad to his school where he was teaching during the day. While he was busy, his pupils often played with me in the forest."

A memorable event came to mind as we were strolling. I had a happy childhood, at least before the Cultural Revolution that began in 1966 and lasted for about ten years. There was a time, three years into the revolution, when Mao called on educated youth and intellectuals mostly from cities to go to the countryside and factories to learn from farmers and workers. According to Mao, the urban educated classes should change their bourgeois outlook into a proletarian one. They needed to practice self-criticism and be re-educated by doing manual labor among poor farmers and factory workers. In the summer of 1969, I was informed that I would have to leave home for Inner Mongolia. I was directed to join a group of youths to do manual labor there. I had no other choice; everyone in my school had to go. The journey was open ended and could turn into a permanent stay. I was sixteen then. One hot summer afternoon, a few weeks before being sent away, sitting on a hard wooden chair in my bedroom, Dad held my hands sobbing like a baby. I had never seen a grown up crying like that in my entire life. I sat on Dad's legs and broke down in tears that were rolling down my cheek like a stream. I didn't know what to say and had few words of comfort for Dad at that moment. I wished I could find a way to tell him that I was going to be alright in Inner Mongolia, but the truth was, in my heart I wasn't sure what my fate was going to be. I knew that any words that I could think of saying would neither be able to comfort our sorrowful souls, nor stop our tears. None of us were able to control our destiny. I still had to go, no matter how hard we cried our eyes out. All schools and universities in the entire country were closed. No one knew how long the revolution was going to last, or what lay ahead of us. It seemed that there was no light at the end of the long tunnel. The image of that afternoon with Dad still flashes vividly through my mind. Neither of us at that moment in time could have pictured us together on foreign soil, let alone coming to America.

Dad's pace was steady, but extremely slow. Along the way he was often out of breath and had to pause to take a rest. I charged ahead for a little while and then had to stop to wait for Dad to catch up. After a few daily rounds of waiting for Dad to catch up, I learned how to match my pace to his. As a young man in his thirties and forties, Dad was always in a hurry, rushing from place to place. At that time he was slim. Being the man in the house, we had depended on him. "Why are you always running? Couldn't you just walk?" Mom shouted to Dad. "I have a lot to do," said Dad. Dad was not a natural born runner, but he had to move fast and get things done for us. Twenty-four hours in a day weren't enough for Dad. He had to run and run faster. He was indeed a man of action.

As for me, in terms of speed of life style, I am neither a runner nor a real walker. I have never enjoyed running, though I once jogged regularly around the state building in the capital of Nebraska, a quick fix for me in an effort to trim my gradually enlarging body back into a slender figure after exposing myself to various cheeses and beef in my first year after coming to America. However, I quit jogging after few months. People who like running must have special DNA to endure what I perceive as a hardship. I believe there are better ways to get fit; one of them is swimming, which to my way of thinking, has additional therapeutic and relaxation benefits.

Time is measured by minutes, hours, days, and years. If one takes no notice, it goes by faster than any rapid swimming or running, faster than anyone can imagine. Somehow Dad and I survived and made it through the Cultural Revolution. Dad now was approaching his eighties. I had already spent half of my life on this foreign soil. As a young man Dad was always in a hurry. Now every step that he took was an effort. He could no longer keep up with me. Dad and I walk at different paces and have different outlooks on life. His generation has slowed down; the baby boomers I belong to are catching up, and soon will pass and leave his generation behind. For the time being, Dad and I were walking together at the same pace on the same country road.

"I hope you will like it here, Dad. My home is yours. I hope you will stay," I said.

"Let's keep walking. I hope I can live until ninety-nine years of age," Dad said, patting me on my right shoulder.

4. To Camp or Not to Camp

Camping with Dad in Oregon

It was still bright and clear after supper. The hot and dry summer afternoon had turned into a mild and comfortable dusk. Dad and I went for a walk in the neighborhood. Our discussion that day was about our recent camping trip to Diamond Lake in southern Oregon.

"What a great trip we had! I'd like to camp again next summer," I said.

"No more camping for me; I will stay home if you decide to camp again," Dad reacted quickly.

"You don't understand a word of English. You can't stay home by yourself," I disagreed.

"I can take care of myself." Dad was determined.

Before meeting Terry, I had never camped in my life. The concept of taking a vacation that involved staying outdoors in a flimsy and drafty tent seemed absurd, since it was not a part of our tradition in China. Terry, a native of the west, is considered a "white ghost" or a "big nose", among my folks in China. Obviously, different strokes for different folks. The western civilization and culture that he belongs to are quite different from mine. According to the eastern view, man is a component of nature. In fact the Chinese word for nature is "zi ran", which literally translates to "self-like", implying that nature is a self-running process and that man is part of nature. This is in sharp contrast to the western view, which often treats nature as a work product that has been built by a creator, and that nature is a force in opposition to mankind. Many cultures have beliefs that assert that nature is created by God. In this belief system, man needs to find his inner self in nature so that he can be closer to God. After the movie Avatar was released, the *San Jose Mercury*, a local newspaper, reported that the resident film critics in the Vatican and its media had criticized the movie for "trying to turn ecology into a religion of millennium...Nature is no longer a creation to defend, but a divinity to worship...a notion the Pope has warned against."

Terry put the idea of camping into my head soon after we met in Nebraska. What was all the fuss about camping? You had a house that you didn't want to live in and a comfortable bed that you didn't wish to sleep in at night. You preferred to sleep on hard ground outdoors in a flimsy tent or even under the stars. What was more, preparation before a camping trip could be brutal. You had to round up all the items on your camping checklist, which included your food, recipes, tent, hiking gear, cooking equipment, flashlights, air mattresses, sleeping bags, and all manner of camping essentials needed for your trip. If you had children, you would have to throw some camping games and toys in your vehicle. There is a lot of effort involved even before you step out of the door. Frankly, I didn't enjoy my first camping weekend with Terry. The morning after my first night outdoors, my neck hurt and my back was sore as a result of sleeping on the ground that was as hard as nails after the air mattress had gone flat. I was cranky. On the contrary, Terry felt reborn and exhilarated.

Later, we moved to the West Coast, home to several well-known national and state parks. Terry now wished to camp even more often. I made a deal with him. If we had to camp every summer, I'd have to get a small tent trailer. I am the kind of person who can't sleep on hard ground outdoors for more than two nights. To hard-core campers, using a tent trailer in the wilderness is considered cheating; it does wonders for me. I have a comfortable bed to sleep on and a potty chair to use during freezing nights. I am well equipped. I have actually learned to enjoy camping as long as I can get hold of a shower. Believe it or not, I've begun to appreciate the outdoors. To camping lovers, perhaps, any degree of preparation before each trip will be worth the effort. Detached from instant texting and emails, out of range of TV, a computer, internet, cell phone, and iPad, even just for a few days, they must feel that the result of all that effort is rewarded by being close to woods, rivers, lakes, mountains, and perhaps the ocean. The Zen-like surroundings bring their mind and soul closer to the nature of God. They find peace and spirit within. As an amateur, with the help of our tent trailer I am willing to search for the same spirit.

Dad had never camped for vacations. He wasn't sure if he wanted to join us on a camping trip at first, but decided to come along after I convinced him that the trip would be surprisingly comfortable, especially with a tent trailer. I'll give him credit for being willing to take a risk. The camping trip took a place in early August. Our plan was to stay on the shore of Diamond Lake, near Crater Lake in Oregon, for two weeks. When we arrived at the lake site campground, we quickly found out that the site we had reserved wasn't up to Dad's standards. "There aren't enough lights. We don't have a concrete area to set up the trailer or to park the car," and "there aren't any paved sidewalks," complained Dad.

We had the tent cranked up, the beds made, and were settled down at our camp site before sunset. By the time we had finished supper, the sky had already turned dark grey. While Terry was putting the food supplies and the camp stove into a bear-proof cage provided by the campground, Dad lit a campfire. Like a child, he enjoyed the process of lighting the fire and watching it take off. He was constantly playing with the fire, flipping the burning wood back and forth and trying to make the flames even bigger and brighter. The orange flames dancing happily in the fire pit brightened Dad's smiling face. Sitting by her grandpa, Celine was content after chomping down several overcooked marshmallows. By the fire, Terry and I studied a trail map and decided to go on a baby hike the next morning. We then all headed to bed dreaming of pleasant hikes and scenery for the next day.

We woke up to a gorgeous morning with a clear, blue sky. The ponderosa pines nearby emitted a sweet and fresh scent of vanilla into the air. After a quick breakfast we packed some snacks and filled our water bottles, then headed to the trailhead where we had planned to hike. We left the car at a wooded parking lot in front of the trailhead. It was an easy two mile loop. According to the trail map, we would first hike to a meadow and end up at a lake before returning. We started out at a slow pace from the beginning of the trail. Dad remained extremely quiet. As we walked further into the woods, the only sounds that I could hear were the echoes of footsteps left behind. "Where are all the people?" I suddenly heard Dad muttering beside me. I turned around and saw his facial coloration turning pale; a childish fear appeared on his face. From his body language, I detected uneasiness. His hesitation sent a strong signal of fear for the wilderness that he was heading to. "We will return soon," I said to Dad and promised him that he wasn't going to be attacked by a protective mother bear or a hungry mountain lion. Without responding, Dad remained silent for the rest of our hiking trip that day.

I can understand why Dad was afraid of the unknown, but I am not sure where his fear of hiking in the woods came from. I can't comprehend a man like Dad, who grew up in a mountain village and was used to playing in the forest as a child, who had walked for a month to join the Red Army in Yan'an and had even been on the long march with Mao, yet was afraid of hiking in the woods. It couldn't be his lack of experience in living in the wilderness. Could the source of his fear be his lack of understanding of blending in as a part of nature? Or perhaps the phenomenon of camping and hiking for a vacation was too foreign to him and he wasn't comfortable with the idea. Maybe what Dad really preferred was a nice vacation in a five-star hotel in a metropolitan city or on a resort island. I had seen his mouth wide open and his eyes beaming with a joy as we drove through the coastal cities of Oregon. Or perhaps Dad was simply getting old and wasn't into any adventures any more. It is said that the older you get, the more childish you become. It is unclear to me why childish behavior increases as one gets older. Is it due to the decline of one's brain and body? If this was true, the world was surely dominated by the childish majority, the youngsters, and the elders (baby boomers are now dominating the census figures). The in-betweens would be the minority. For now I was happy to be the minority. For once on this hike, I didn't want to confront Dad, nor did I wish to treat him like a child.

We planned another hike on the second day. This time we were heading to the mountaintop near the campsite.

"The air pressure is high up there. Can't breath. Not good for my heart," said Dad.

"You can rest by the lake. You don't have to go." I offered him an alternative.

Dad took the advice and stayed behind. He never hiked with us again during the rest of the trip. The August climate in that area of Oregon is normally warm during the day and cool at night, but it can also change dramatically without any warning. One day it started drizzling and rained on and off like cats and dogs during the second week of our stay. The rain and the wet ground lowered the temperature in the area. Inside the tent trailer we were cold, especially at night, so we provided Dad with an extra blanket on top of his heavy-duty sleeping bag. During the day we provided him with another layer in the form of a sweater. Dad became increasingly restless. "We are still here. Most people have already left the campground," he said with a look of a concern after a couple of heavy overnight rain events. This observation was indeed true, as many of the campers who were staying in tents on bare ground had been flooded out and had fled the campsite with their soaked belongings. However, due to our tent trailer being a few feet above ground, we were high and dry. The fact that about half the campers had left added to the appeal of the campsite, since we now had more space and facilities to ourselves. Dad, however, did not share our enthusiasm for the situation and spent the last few days of our adventure either inside the trailer or in the warm lobby of a nearby lodge.

One day while driving back to the campsite from a visit to the Lava Center, we spotted a Chinese restaurant on the road side. This discovery generated unexpected excitement from Dad. We decided to have supper there. The place was small, dreary, and empty, but clean. The waitress greeted us politely in broken English. We ordered fried rice, a bowl of noodle soup, and a few stir-fried dishes to share. The portions of these dishes were huge, but the flavors were plain. The waitress must have known we were hungry. Indeed, we were. It was a special treat after eating food prepared on a camp stove every night. The taste of the food wasn't judged or criticized by Dad that night. We went for the quantity and paid little attention to the quality presented to us. It was a feast. That restaurant magically lifted Dad's spirit in a way that no lava caves or exhibitions of igneous, sedimentary, and metamorphic rocks ever could.

What did I do to my poor dad, I pondered as I lay in my sleeping bag in the tent trailer that night. My intention for the whole trip was to show Dad a different stimulating part of America; hopefully, in response he would appreciate the beauty of the land. My intention and the reality of the situation didn't go together and I had failed. Dad obviously didn't enjoy camping in the least. Is camping really too uncivilized for him? I wonder if his longing for comfort was stronger than his desire to witness the beauty of nature. People do not always see eye to eye. The concept of being comfortable could be interpreted in different ways. Dad's definition of comfort and mine were noticeably different. This couldn't be the same person who marched for hundreds of miles on foot from his rural village all the way to Yan'an, according to "Symbol of the Chinese Revolution" published by *China.org.cn*, is where the Red Army was based, and where the "Chinese [C] communists sought to realize their idealized vision of life, culture, and social justice." Thus the significance of Yan'an is that this city, even today, represents a "golden age when communist principles and ideals were actively pursued by many sincere, youthful supporters."

Dad was no stranger to hard times and rough living conditions. Dad's given name is Yong Da, meaning forever reaching. He was born in the Wei village (*Wei Jia Tan*) located in the suburb of Xin County of Shanxi Province in China. My grandparents passed away when Dad was only seven years old. It was the darkest time in his life. Dad left his home town at the age of twelve and joined the Red Army. "There was immense sorrow in my heart. Imagine, my mother passed away, and two years after that my dad died," he said to me one day as we were pacing up our neighborhood road. "The reason I left earlier was because of the harsh conditions at home," he went on. Dad was too young to help out on the family farm. Learning about Dad's situation, his fourth uncle, who was already in the Red Army, sent a letter to the village asking if Dad could join him in Yan'an, Shaanxi Province. With his youngest uncle, Dad left the village for good. They started a long journey by foot. They stopped at a relative's home on the first night and moved on after a few days. At the beginning, they carried enough food with them, but later the food ran out before they reached to their final destination. While walking up to eighteen miles each day, they found shelter at the villagers' homes during the night along the way. The villagers trusted them and let them stay overnight even though they were strangers. They provided dinner and sent them off after breakfast the next morning. It took Dad and his uncle about a month to reach Yan'an.

Sleepless in the tent trailer by the shore of Diamond Lake, I was searching for a clue or for any correlation between this camping trip and Dad's march to Yan'an. Why was he able to march for a long distance then, amid discomfort and hunger? Yet he couldn't endure mild hiking or easy camping now. To survive, Dad had to leave home at a young age. The survival instinct had to be the motivation for him to march. Times had changed. Decades after that march, Dad had perhaps reached a certain stage of his life in which anything uncomfortable or uncultivated by the human touch of was no longer an interest of his. The meaning of comfort depends on whom you talk to. The concept of familiarity is inseparable to the particular society and culture one belongs to. Comfort is relative to the environment one lives in. Familiarity correlates with comfort. One feels secure in a familiar setting. Familiarity and security go hand in hand. One finds comfort in a secure environment. Having both, one feels more confident. The notion of camping for a vacation was foreign to Dad. He had neither security nor confidence on this trip. During the last decade, living conditions in China have improved tremendously. People there have more money and live a better life. The society Dad was familiar with has changed forever. Perhaps to Dad comfort, whether it is material or mental, has become more important in the new era. Maybe his view towards camping, hiking, or nature in general differs from mine fundamentally (admittedly, my own view of camping has changed after many years out in nature with Terry). Dad has never elaborated nor offered me his thoughts about camping in the wilderness. Perhaps he doesn't want to say anything to hurt my feelings.

People come with different shapes, sizes, and beliefs, no matter where they are from or what their culture is. There is extraordinary diversity in the human race and we often stereotype an individual group and the culture within. Quite a few westerners I know aren't fond of camping or outdoor activities either. Psychologically, to some of my Chinese friends nature in its raw and uncultivated form seems to be dangerous, threatening, unhealthy, or dirty. In this paradigm, civilized people do not cook and sleep out in the wilderness. Yoshiko Nomura, a Japanese educator, states that the Eastern view of nature is that "man is a part of nature". Yoshiko thinks of the Western view of nature as diametrically opposed with "nature as a separate force from man." In recent years, however, the west has moved closer to eastern thinking in this respect, which is apparent in areas such as the science of ecology, the environmental movement, architecture, landscape architecture, health, and philosophy. I wonder if Dad unconsciously falls into a group of people who believe that human life needs to be improved continuously through nature; that the improved human life is measured by the conditions that men live in, not by nature itself.

Definitely there is a generation gap here in viewing camping and its relationship with nature. The physical comfort factor also plays a large part. As Dad ages, hiking and camping in the wilderness becomes a more physically demanding task. Do people in his generation feel they are physically incapable? The cultural view of aging in China is that once you have reached fifty years old, or perhaps even before that, you are considered to be old and feeble. Yet, on the other hand, to remind people constantly that you are getting old is not necessarily a bad thing psychologically, since Chinese people believe that the older one gets, the wiser one becomes. There is no one shoe size, or one single frame that fits everyone. I have seen healthy seniors climbing to the top of Yosemite falls, nordic skiing in the Sierra, and hiking to high peaks in the Rocky Mountains. They have inspired me; I hope I can be like them when I reach their age. Would it be great if Dad too was inspired by their story? Perhaps Dad's unwillingness had nothing to do with all these factors. Perhaps as a veteran of marching with Mao during the Chinese Civil War, he feels that he has already experienced hiking as marching, and that living outdoors is more of a deprivation than an opportunity to commune with nature. If that is true, then maybe Dad had his fair share of outdoor experiences. He had traveled a long way to reach to this point in his life. It is time for him to enjoy the rest of his life in a way that feels appropriate for him. For Dad, enjoyment means no more camping and hiking. What is wrong with that, as long as he leads a healthy lifestyle?

5. Bowl of Noodles

In March of 2005, Dad returned to California from his several months visit to Beijing. He had put on a few more pounds due to the delicious and more familiar food there, so much so that on the way back home from the San Francisco airport, the only topic on Dad's mind was the food he had during this visit to Beijing. In particular he loved the wonderful bowl of noodles he had in a Shanxi Noodle Restaurant. These noodles had obviously made a huge impression on him; I wondered about the important role of food in our lives, both cultural and nutritional. Dad was comfortable dining there, since the restaurant shared the same name as Shanxi, the province where he was born. I wonder if the owner of that restaurant was really from Shanxi, though. Sometimes a name of a restaurant can be a gimmick, and in reality might have nothing to do with its place of origin or style of cooking that it is named for. This tendency seems to be universal whether in China or America. A few years ago an Asian couple opened a Japanese restaurant in the city where we live. The place was popular. We tried it a few times and were very satisfied with what we had eaten. The sushi was delicious and the sashimi was fresh. Each time, before leaving the restaurant, Terry said something good about the food in his very basic Japanese. In return, the owners always nodded their heads politely with huge grins of acknowledgement. Later on, we found out that the owners weren't from Japan, but from Korea and they didn't understand a word of Japanese!

Back at our central California abode, Dad's previous daily routine resumed, but the topic of his recent conversations remained focused on noodles, which became the topic of discussion during our walk.

"It is not easy to make Shanxi noodles. To make good Shanxi noodles, you have to know peeling, pulling, and kneading techniques," Dad said seriously, while pacing slowly.

"There is a great variety of noodles; Shanxi is famous for its dao xiao mian and la mian," he went on proudly.

"I heard you saying that many times before," I said, trying to be polite.

"But you have never had them in Shanxi Province."

"All noodles seem to be the same wherever you eat."

"Oh, no. This shows that you really know nothing about noodles."

Among the many variations of noodles, Dad's favorite is kneaded noodles (*dao xiao mian* in Chinese). "They are more delicious," said Dad enthusiastically. The recipe for pulled and peeled noodles calls for wheat flour, water, and salt. These noodles are peeled from the dough using a sharp knife and a quick hand. However, buckwheat flour is often used in the kneaded recipe in Shanxi Province rather than using wheat flour. I was curious and wondered why kneaded noodles were so special. I went online and sure enough, I found in *Wikipedia* that "A small ball of dough is lightly rolled on a flat surface until it is several centimeters long and spindle shaped." I fully acknowledged that *Wikipedia* might not be a reliable source of information according to serious scholars. Rolled on a flat surface? But the source didn't elaborate what a kind of flat surface it was made on. It didn't say anything about making it on a surface of a human leg. My memory as a child was of often hearing Mom saying to Dad, "those noodles are kneaded on the dirty legs of villagers in Shanxi. These people never take a shower or have a bath. People there are backward. How can the noodles be that delicious?" Dad would then raise his eyebrows and chuckle with great laughter.

It doesn't matter if noodles come in different shapes or sizes, nor does it matter if they are prepared in a cold salad or boiled in a hot soup, or if they are deep-fried or stir fried. According to Dad, they are all delicious. Among the various types of noodle dishes, apart from kneaded noodles, Dad's favorites are fried Chinese miso noodles and sesame noodles. On our family table in China, the former tended to be served hot, while the later is a cold dish. When I grew up, my parents never used recipes while preparing food at home. The amount of ingredients that they used to prepare any dishes was utterly dependent on how much they felt was needed at the time, or simply by trial and error. The typical ingredients used by Dad for the sauce of fried miso noodles normally included cooking oil (could be any kind that he had on hand at the moment), ground pork, green onions, and Chinese miso. He stir-fried them together, then separately cooked the noodles (could be any kind, shape, and size) in boiling water, drained the noodles once they were done, and served the noodles with the sauce on top. After eating Dad's miso noodles repeatedly for a while, even Mom began to complain of excess noodles. "I could make a much better noodle dish if I were able to see," Mom said to Dad one day.

Cold sesame noodles, on the other hand, seemed to be more tolerable to Mom and me. Dad made it a couple of times while he was in the States, especially on a hot summer day. He turned a classic Chinese sesame paste, warm water, and salt into a noodle sauce. Cooked cold noodles served with the sauce are fantastic with ham, cucumber, and cilantro. It is a nice meal all by itself. Dad's version of a cold sesame noodle dish contains:

- Chinese sesame paste (the amount depends on the final consistency desired)

- Warm water

- Lots of salt, depending upon individual taste and tolerance

- Smoked ham

- 1 cucumber (can be any kind)

- Fresh diced cilantro

- Chinese noodles (any kind), boiled, drained and rinsed with cold water

Directions:

- Stir the first three ingredients together and make them into a thin watery sauce

- Slice through some smoked ham horizontally (Slices less than ½ inch)

- Slice 1 cucumber (can be any kind) vertically (Slices less than ½ inch)

- Garnish with diced fresh cilantro

- Add all of the above to any kind of Chinese noodles

The truth is Dad loves them all. He has an ability to eat any kind of Chinese noodles three times a day and thirty days a month without blinking an eye or getting bored. Perhaps everyone has his or her favorite food. I don't know how and why noodles became Dad's go-to meal, other than the fact that Dad is from Shanxi where well-known noodles are produced. In the old days, food was scarce and the villagers were poor. One reason for the popularity of noodles was that noodles that contain basically wheat, water, and salt were affordable and simple to make. In the mountainous region of Shanxi, nothing grew well except for wheat and buckwheat. If there wasn't enough wheat, then buckwheat was the replacement. Nothing could be better than having a bowl of warm buckwheat noodle soup in winter or a cold bowl in a hot summer. Maybe this is a good enough reason to love noodles. Or perhaps finding your favorite food is like being in a Bingo game. You get a right number and you win. Sometimes you win big. Winning big can get you emotionally high and arouse a feeling of excitement that gives you comfort and security. I suppose noodles provide Dad with the same kind of emotion and security that Bingo winners have. He finds great consolation in a bowl of noodles, similar to the consolation that one finds after drinking a glass of good wine. The way Dad is hooked on noodles is like smokers' addiction to nicotine. Chinese noodles aren't something that Dad can give up easily.

There are many types of Chinese noodles that one can discover in the Asian restaurants and markets in the United States. Although we had searched high and low, Dad and I hadn't yet found a nearby restaurant that specializes in Shanxi kneaded noodles. Maybe we didn't look hard enough.

Unfortunately there were no Asian food markets on our side of the coastal mountains. Dad had to lower his standards and cook any type of noodles that we could get from the local Safeway, Nob Hill, or other grocery store. We dined at a few local Chinese restaurants, but the noodles there were no comparison to those in Beijing. After trying spaghetti once at a local Italian restaurant, Dad decided that he wasn't going to allow any Italian noodles to get into his stomach again. "Chinese noodles are much better than Italian noodles. Marco Polo copied the recipe from China, but somehow when translated back in Italy, they got it wrong," he declared, then followed up with an argument about who was the first inventor of noodles. Dad's remarks about Marco Polo seemed to be true but I wondered if Italians believe they are the copy cats. To investigate the matter further, I conducted a quick online search. Based on the Chinese Noodles section of *Museum of Learning: Explore a Virtual Museum of Knowledge*, the result revealed history records stating that, "although the Chinese, Arabs, and Italians have all claimed to have been the first to create noodles, the first written account of noodles dates from the Chinese East Han Dynasty, between AD 25 and 220." History is on Dad's side. China is indeed the birthplace of noodles.

I like noodles now, but as a child I wasn't so keen on them. One incident occurred when Mom was out of town on business. My brother and I were home alone with Dad, who was the main chef for two weeks. It was our first taste of Dad's serious cooking in action. We ended up eating his watery noodles every night. In order to protect myself from an assault of tasteless noodles, I decided that action must be taken to prevent further exposure to pale strips of wheat. So one day I feigned a stomachache right after supper. After that, Dad's cooking finally shifted in response to my defense strategy.

Whenever my parents would plan noodles for dinner, I said to them that I was going to have tummy aches again if we were having those noodles. The toughest challenge for me to escape a meal of noodles was on my birthdays. My parents insisted that I had to have noodles along with some boiled eggs on my birthday each year. They said noodles represented a long life; boiled eggs were symbols of fruition, symbolic of the number of children that one was able to have in life. Now I wonder if I truly will have a long life ahead. In terms of children, I am not sure how much magic the birthday eggs did for me. I only have one child. At any rate, I tried my best to escape the noodle situation and I was usually successful, except for special occasions like birthdays.

My parents told me that I should feel lucky enough to have noodles on the dinner table compared with millions of people who died of starvation during the Three Years of Natural Disasters outside Beijing. It is also called "The Great Chinese Famine" which lasted from 1959 to 1961. There are different views on why and how the famine started and became widespread. After touring the country, Mao had concluded that the people of China had the ability to achieve anything and the two primary goals that he felt they should aim for were success in industry and agriculture. In 1958 Mao made a public announcement of a second Five Year Plan that was called the Great Leap Forward. To westerners, the Great Leap Forward movement, accompanied by China's inner policy changes, had triggered the devastating disaster. As a child I remember hearing that during the Great Leap Forward the peasants had to melt their farming tools into metal for industrialization, thus leaving them with little means to grow crops. I was holding a bowl of noodles and should feel fortunate compared with others in China.

When I was born, my parents were working for a branch office of Xinhua News Agency (the only government press in China at the time) in Wu Han, a city along the Yangtze River, the longest river in Asia and the third-longest in the world. They were transferred to Xinhua's headquarters in Beijing in 1960. During that period the grocery store shelves in Beijing were almost empty. We had the basics: wheat or rice with very limited choices of vegetables for dinner. I remember not having any meat in my rice or noodle bowl for a long time. Distribution of all food supplies was controlled by the government. Sometimes Dad would bring home a bag of soy beans or a bag of pure sugar distributed to him by the agency. A memorable event comes to mind regarding Mom's craving for dumplings. She couldn't find any vegetables for sale in any local stores she went to. On that day Dad came home with a half eggplant distributed to him. Mom used the eggplant for the filling. Usually dumpling filling is made of chopped pork, beef, chicken, and shrimp mixed with chopped vegetables. Mom created eggplant dumplings without using anything else, which was unheard of. She didn't complain; it turned out to be one of the happiest days for her. What an inventor! Even a fussy eater like Mom was forced to grin and bear it in that situation. The memory of having those eggplant dumplings has stuck in my head for a long time. Whenever I think about it, I can still taste the bitterness of those dumplings.

Unlike Dad, I don't have the "it" factor. Although, when I was pregnant with Celine I craved greasy, but delicious Chinese doughnuts (*you tiao* in Chinese). As matter of a fact, I always liked you tiao with soybean milk for breakfast as a child. Chinese breakfast is not as boring as many westerners think when visiting China. You tiao, a long string of lightly salted wheat dough deep fried in oil, is one of the favorite breakfast delights among northern Chinese. It was typically served with a bowl of steaming hot soy milk back then. I didn't have the luxury to have it often. If I had an opportunity to have this golden-brown bread stick with a bowl of soy milk in the morning, it certainly made my day. However, I don't consider it as my "it", not like noodles, the "it" Dad has. In the States I can go without thinking about you tiao for days, months, or years, except when I was pregnant. At home in California, the closest place to find Chinese doughnuts was at the food court in the Chinese supermarket forty-five minutes away. I made Terry drive there several times during my pregnancy.

My family belongs to the tea house culture. Business deals are made in tea houses in China instead of at coffee houses. At home in Beijing, we drank tea religiously. I recall that jasmine was the favorite tea after each meal. It took me two years to get used to the taste of coffee after coming to the U.S. The coffee business is enormous in America. One gets dizzy just thinking about the vast number of varieties of coffee beans and types of coffee drinks. There is an art of choosing the right coffee drink. Espresso, latte, or mocha? Americano, cappuccino, or frappuccino? Doubleshot or single? Caffeinated or decaf? Shade or sun grown? Organic or regular? Fair price or commercial? Even more daunting is choosing the right coffee house. Surf City? Starbucks or Peets? Coffee culture is now deeply rooted in America. I still haven't had a chance to sample many different types of coffee drinks. I'll stick with latte and house coffee for now.

"Pizza is Americans' favorite," I was told by a friendly fellow who had emigrated from Hong Kong. One day during my first year in Omaha, Nebraska, the fellow invited me and several other Chinese students to dine in a local pizza parlor. I wasn't amused by the flattened disk of bread dough that we ate; I couldn't understand why pizza was such a big deal, a signature cuisine to Americans. Years later, I finally got it. It's one dimensional, but easy to cook and delicious. It also comes with a variety of toppings. Pizza is a type of food that one can quickly get, quickly eat, and be quickly done. It fits the instant gratification lifestyle of this country, quick and on the go. Of course, to Dad there was nothing special about it. If Dad absolutely had to eat American food, he would willingly eat pizza with no complaints. According to him, Italians basically copied and learned how to make pizza from the Chinese centuries ago, just as they had copied noodles.

When I think of the food that I had in Nebraska, I think of the American traditions on the Great Plains. Nebraska, as a leading ranching state of the country, is not only famous for its Cornhusker college football team, but also well-known for its fresh, tender steak and hearty corn. By some accounts it has more millionaire farmers and ranchers than any other state. I learned to enjoy Nebraska cheese and steak too much; at one point, I had gained more pounds that I wished. I eventually got to the point that for the sake of good health I had to jog around the state capital building in Lincoln three times a week in order to trim my sails.

When I think of the food that I have enjoyed in California, I think of a variety of ethnic cuisines. There are stories about cross-cultural perspectives on eating behaviors among different ethnic groups. Theories of food, culture, and society are also examined and debated by food and social scientists. *The Encyclopedia of Food & Culture* points out that, "the development of food likes and dislikes reflects the operation of" factors such as genetics, "maternal diet, child rearing practices, learning, cognition, and culture. The development of food preferences" involves "the interplay of these influences during our life span." As I am thinking about food and culture, a memory flashes in my mind during my parents' visit for three months in 1991. During their entire stay, they only ate Chinese food. It was the food they were used to, that they loved; no other cuisine could compare with it. The closest Asian market, called Marina, was thirty miles away "over the hill", as we locals like to say. Without an Asian market close by, it was a challenge to find all the supplies and ingredients that my parents wanted on a weekly basis. Our trip to Marina was usually taken once a month. When we went, we normally loaded up with Chinese greens, tofu, prepared dumplings, steamed bread, and Chinese noodles; enough for a month. My parents returned from Marina not only with plenty of goods, but also with huge smiles and bundled excitement. Somehow Marina made them feel closer to their home in Beijing. In the crowd of Asian shoppers, they felt a sense of belonging. It seemed as if they felt they had never left their home. Tofu, dumplings, and noodles seemed to taste better from Marina than from our local super markets. To my parents, shopping over the hill was a big cultural and social occasion somewhat akin to attending a concert or an opera.

Every afternoon during their stay, my parents sat at our dinner table, preparing dinner for a few hours. They chatted with laughter while hand making noodles and steamed bread from scratch, and took pleasure in their production efforts wholeheartedly. "We had fun making these noodles and streamed breads," Mom said to me joyfully. Dad nodded his head in agreement. In this strange country they found comfort in making Chinese food together. The work of making dinner reminded them of their own cultural background. As for me, I was only too happy to find my dinner always ready after coming back from work, bless their hearts. I felt grateful in the beginning. However, a month into eating the same kind of food day in and day out, I got tired of it and longed for an alteration in the pattern. Unlike my childhood strategy of feigning illness, I didn't reject their cooking, nor did I say a word about it. I didn't wish to hurt their feelings. After all, they were visitors from thousands of miles away. Later on, after my parents were gone, I couldn't touch any Chinese food for three months.

This time, twelve years after my parents' first visit, Dad had returned alone. He held a Green Card and was no longer considered a visitor. Could he develop a sense of taste for American food? I introduced Dad to a variety of cuisines in many local restaurants where he could sample distinct styles of cooking. We tried Japanese, Mexican, Italian, Indian, Thai, Greek, Vietnamese, and traditional American. In the end Dad decided that he only liked pizza. Costco pizza won the lottery and found a special place in Dad's heart. Freshly made and reasonably priced, Costco pizza reminded him Chinese pancakes. I also think that eating our freshly cooked pizza at the crowded Costco tables while watching the shoppers drift in and out of the store fondly reminded him of the bustling hordes of people present where he usually ate out in Beijing.

In general I am not a good chef. If I cooked a Chinese dish, it was never good enough by Dad's standard. Anything I cooked that didn't taste like what he had in China was western to him. One day after I had prepared dinner for us, while we were pacing through the neighborhood, Dad said to me,

"I don't like western food."

"What do you mean, Dad? Didn't I just cook you up a Chinese stir fry?"

"That wasn't real Chinese."

"We will have to get real Chinese at the food court in Marina, then."

"You can cook whatever you want. I just want to have some Chinese noodles," said Dad. "You know, I can have noodles for lunch and have no problem to have them again for dinner," he went on.

As I listened to Dad, I realized that a bowl of Chinese noodles was the only kind of food Dad really loved here in America. No Italian or other ethnic cuisine could take its place, no matter how expensive or tasty they might be. He occasionally accepted Costco pizza, only because it looked like Chinese pancake. That was about it.

This experience has taught me some lessons about food preferences. I realize now that in addition to the sensory properties of food –taste, flavor, and texture –there is a cultural overlay which imparts strong biases over our immediate perceptions. In my father's case, his cultural attachments and associations with Chinese noodles were too strong to overcome my admonitions and enticements to try various western foods that I thought would be delicious. One cannot try to substitute or improve upon a simple bowl of noodles that is steeped in the sauces of memory and culture.

6. Pookie and Cooper

Pookie in our backyard

I grew up without any pets. Cats and dogs weren't allowed in the cities. I had accepted that fact and had never asked for a pet. One day Dad came home with a turtle he got from his business trip. He didn't know what genus or species it was, or what kind of habitat it needed. "It is from the southern part of the country," was the only information Dad could offer to us. He poured some water into a glass bowl that became the turtle's new home. Shortly after it settled down, the little turtle mysteriously disappeared. We had no idea how the turtle had got out of the bowl. We never found it again.

People raised chickens and roosters in Wu Han, south of the Yangtze River, the place where I was born. Nicknamed "the furnace", Wu Han is well-known for its unbearably hot and humid summers. We lived in a residential area where people all knew each other, and all worked for the Xinhua News Agency, the only official press in the entire country. On oppressive muggy summer nights, it was impossible to stay inside houses that had no air conditioning. To cool off, my parents often moved the family bamboo beds to the backyard after supper and the whole family would sleep outdoors overnight. The backyard was also shared by other residents working for the agency. It was fun for me to sleep outside with other kids, along with chickens and roosters in such an open way. The residential yard was huge; we had room to run around, chase each other, and play hide and seek after dinner.

One early evening I was eating a snack on the bamboo mat in the yard. There weren't many people outside yet. A proud rooster walked towards me defiantly, stopping in front of my bamboo bed. His little head moved up and down, side to side, examining my snack thoroughly. Suddenly and unexpectedly, the rooster jumped onto me and tried to take away my snack. I panicked. My only response was to run away as fast as I could. I started running round and round in a circle. The rooster didn't give up and persistently chased after me. After a few rounds I got tired, but the rooster was still following right behind. I got very scared and cried out. Dad heard me and rushed outside. "Drop the snack," he instructed. While the rooster was gobbling up the snack, he chased it away. My recollection of the encounter with that rooster haunted me for years after that.

In my juvenile years, most city dwellers didn't own any pets that were bigger than a bird. I was told there wasn't enough space for cats and dogs in the cities, particularly in the crowded capital city of Beijing. There weren't any established rules or regulations for pet owners, either. In the countryside, farmers were allowed to have farm animals including pets such as rabbits, cats, and dogs. Dogs on farms were raised and trained as watch dogs. When I heard the word "watch", with the word "dog", I smelled danger and trouble. Watch dogs were portrayed in many scary tales and reputedly would bite, attack, and hunt you down without fear. This perception is somewhat akin to over-reactions towards the pit bull terrier in the U.S. nowadays. Many people think that it is not safe to be anywhere near one of them.

When I was stationed in Inner Mongolia during the Cultural Revolution, I had the misfortune to meet my match in a watch dog. One cold mid-afternoon in winter, I was returning on foot from the farm headquarters to the village where I lived and labored. The one way trip was about one and a half hours. Normally for a trip like this, because of the distance and potential hazards, I would have a companion. But on that day I was alone. I started out under a clear sky and a brightly shining sun. The crops in the fields had long since been harvested. The frozen fields covered with dust and colored blond by the sunlight were singing with the same rhythm as the chilly wind was breezing through. The endless fields, connected with one another, stretched far into the distant horizon. Along the way I was accompanied not by *Homo sapien* companions, but by the mountain range far away with grey and brown peaks rising abruptly from the Earth's surface, standing tall and straight above the Mongolian Plateau. Because these mountains were far way, they did not seem to be moving away or getting closer, and I had the impression that they were like faithful companions, always near me. Were they the Altai Mountains that cover a vast region including Russia, Kazakhstan, China and Mongolia? I wondered if the Gobi Desert, the fifth largest desert in the world, was on the other side of the mountain range. Did this desert divide Outer Mongolia from Inner Mongolia? "White clouds floating in the blue sky; horses are running under the clouds..." I couldn't help singing one of my favorite folk songs about Mongolia as I walked. The song that I learned in my elementary years evoked a mystical and romantic attitude toward the region. Was there grassland covered with white sheep over the ridge? Was Outer Mongolia indeed as beautiful and romantic as the lyrics in the folk song suggested? There was not a single soul on the lonely road in the countryside that I could share my thoughts with. I could only hear the wind singing and feel its chill sting my frozen face and ears. Half way into my journey, a small village gradually appeared in the distance. I could see white smoke lifting into the sky from the chimneys of the rural huts. The sun started sinking behind the village and below the surface of the Earth as I approached. An eerie silence surrounded the village; there was no one on the streets as I passed. A memory of stories about vicious watch dogs flashed back and forth in my mind. I was scared but mentally prepared for any watch dogs approaching my direction. But I didn't spot any dogs, nor did I hear any barks. I said to myself this might be my lucky day as I quickly and quietly passed through the silent buildings of the village. Just as I was coming to the edge of the village, I suddenly sensed something behind me; I was being followed. I turned around and saw a dog, perhaps a watch dog, running towards me. My heart jumped and started pumping fast. There I was, totally on my own on the empty streets. What should I do? Nobody could help me out. Was the dog going to bite me? Run, run fast, my brain was telling me. The dog sped up and chased after me as I was running away from the village. Just as I was about to cry out for help, I spotted a lone stone on the dirt road side. This stone was my last hope to stop the dog, I thought. I bent down, picked it up, and threw it hard at the dog a few steps away. The stone fell to one side of the dog, but, to my surprise, it stopped its pursuit. The dog stared at me for a few seconds, then turned around and left me alone. That was my first close encounter with a watch dog. It was a miracle and as I continued walking I drew pride in knowing I had a new *Indiana Jones* story to tell when I arrived home.

For many years, into my adulthood, I was timid around dogs. I tried to hide or go in different directions if I encountered one on a street. If I couldn't hide, I would just stand still, trying to wait it out or let it pass by while pretending to be cool. The trouble is that it is very hard to avoid dogs in public places in America. Dogs are the number one beloved pets in the country, I am told. Dogs are cute and adorable to look at in pictures, as long as they don't go near me. While in Beijing, a city that once outlawed dogs and now permits its people to have dogs, Dad went to different dog shows and enjoyed them all. After that, he got a dog as a gift from my brother. But it peed, barked, and chewed the furniture in the house. As a result, Dad gave it away to a friend after having it only for a few months. "Too much trouble," complained Dad to me during a long distance call from Beijing. He wanted the dog to be his source of pleasure or amusement without the realization that it needed training. He had no idea how to train a dog, nor did he know where he could get a trainer or help. I thought with this limited experience at least, Dad wouldn't be timid around dogs.

In the States, our neighborhood dogs increasingly gave Dad headaches during our daily walks. Occasionally Dad and I ran into a dog without a leash on the road or we came across our neighbors who were walking with their dogs. My reaction to these dogs was cool; I just kept calm and natural. Dad's was the opposite. If he saw one, he immediately became stiff as a board and the look on his face would turn serious and distraught. One day a neighbor was walking by with her two little dogs. As we passed by her, the dogs began to bark and jump at us. "Stupid dogs. Trouble makers," Dad cried out angrily in Chinese. While the owner was trying to control the dogs, Dad turned around, interrupted his walk, and quickly returned to the house. I hadn't seen him moving so fast for a long time. Back in the house, Dad didn't mention a word about the dogs again and tried to act composed, as if nothing had happened.

Cooper came into my life by chance. One of my colleagues at the university had committed to train a guide dog. With management permission, on one mid-winter day my colleague came to the office with a two-and-a-half-month old female puppy, a guide dog in training, named Cooper, a Labrador Retriever with beautiful, lustrous, black fur. I was told she was small and calm in comparison with most labs. From her trainer I had heard several positive stories about these dogs' good behavior. Cooper was as good as one could get. She was sweet and had a good nature; a role model for all dogs. My office was close to her trainer's and conveniently provided me an opportunity to observe and to get to know Cooper. In order to break the ice, once in a while I would hand her one or two dog biscuits. "Tell her to do something for you. Tell her to sit before you give her the biscuits," her trainer suggested. "Cooper, sit," I said softly to her, as if I was talking to a child. Cooper wagged her tail, eyed the biscuits, and obeyed my command eagerly. In an effort to learn more about the species, I borrowed a book about labs that told me that the

Labrador was the most popular breed of dog in many countries. To put what I had learned from the book into practice, I observed Cooper's body language carefully, gently petted and talked to her without alarming her. As the days went by, I began feeling more comfortable being alone with her. I was given opportunities to play and feed Cooper and occasionally to take her outside the office building for her potty breaks. Inside our building, Cooper often wagged her tail and visited me at my desk; she quickly formed a tight bond of obedience and loyalty with me. I fell in love. In my eyes, Cooper became a sweet and gentle baby, no longer a dog, no longer a lower living organism. We were equal in status and quality. Her daily presence, without a doubt, had helped to reduce my level of my anxiety and stress at work.

One day, one and half months into the training, Cooper didn't show up at the office. After my initial surprise and concern, I later learned that Cooper had a knee problem and needed a surgical procedure. As a result of her physical condition, it would no longer be possible for her to be a guide dog. However, she would have a chance to be adopted into a permanent home. I broke down and sobbed like a baby. Fearing to lose her, I seriously considered adopting Cooper. The thought of adopting a dog was a real transformation for someone like me who had recently been terrified of dogs. I wanted Cooper to have a happier life with me. Deep in my heart, I knew I wouldn't be a good candidate to adopt her. The Guide Dog Agency normally selects someone who has an experience with dogs, I was told, and I had none. I pondered what the future was going to be for guide dogs in training, like Cooper, if they had physical issues. To my great relief, my colleague decided to take Cooper under her wing herself. I also received a promise of future invitations to visit her at any time by her new owner. Cooper has changed my life and my feelings about dogs in general. Because of her, I have become a dog lover.

A couple of years before I met Cooper, there were the fish. By the time when Celine reached three, she asked for a pet. With busy working schedules, Terry and I found it hard to decide on the right pet for Celine. It was said that raising fish was easy. Besides, it was said that observing fish swimming in an aquarium had therapeutic value. So we bought some fish for Celine. We bought her a small aquarium with all the usual accessories such as a heater, light, plants, air pump, filter, and thermometer. Then we had to go through the stage of building up the proper aquatic ecosystem in terms of nitrification and microorganisms, at the expense of several unfortunate, sacrificial, cheaper goldfish. Finally we were ready for the high quality, more interesting, but expensive tropical fish. We changed a portion of the water in the fish tank routinely and checked the water temperature several times a week. The brightly colored fish on display in Celine's room were a wonder to behold, and at first we would all make detours into Celine's room to see the fresh water wonders. Unfortunately, perhaps because of our lack of experience, the fish one by one slowly disappeared until one day they were all gone. After the fish we considered other possibilities; having a cat was out of the question, since both Celine and Terry are allergic to cats. Then came the idea of having a dog. It was said that dogs could help people relax and focus their energy away from their daily problems and worries. They could contribute positively to people's health and wellness. However, having a pet dog was not practical. I was told that your child's pet would eventually become yours. In the end, the parents are the ones who ultimately must take care of the family pet. That was not going to happen to us, since we were already overloaded. At an Easter party, the image of a cute bunny jumped into Celine's mind. "What about a rabbit?" she asked. Rabbits spend much of their time feeding and are not as socially demanding as dogs. I agreed that a rabbit would make a great pet for her, so we made the decision.

On a warm August afternoon in 2003, we picked up a female mini rex rabbit from our local pet store. It cost us thirty dollars. I later realized that in the interests of animal welfare we should have adopted a bunny from the local animal shelter, which always has an ample supply of rabbits on hand, already vaccinated and spayed or neutered. But at that time we were unaware of the issues involved. After great deliberation, we named our bunny Pookie after a rabbit in a children's story book that Terry was familiar with, and instantly fell in love with her. She was shy for a few days, not even daring to risk the environment outside her tiny bunny-igloo, but warmed up to us soon after. Our cute and cuddly bunny had velvety, beautiful brown and white fur, milk chocolate eyes, and a constantly twitching nose. It was impossible for us to resist her. She felt so soft and sweet when we were cuddling her. Once Pookie got used to us, she was playful. We would give her free run of the house once in a while and would watch her slip and slide on the hardwood floors, hearing the little clitter–clatter of the nails on her small white paws.

Pookie enjoyed jumping and flipping in a huge cage that Terry had built for her out of the remains of our kitchen remodel project that enabled Pookie to safely play outdoors in the backyard. Often Celine rolled on the ground in the cage with Pookie; her funny behavior made Celine giggle. Either as pure coincidence or in a show of long-eared solidarity, several wild rabbits showed up in our back yard soon after we started putting Pookie outdoors occasionally in the cage to graze upon our lawn. Terry would move the cage around to different pastures throughout the day in an attempt to have Pookie substitute as a lawn mower. The wild rabbits, however, had soon chomped the entire lawn down to the height of a well kept putting green. After the demise of the lush lawn, we would throw carrots to Pookie when she was put outdoors in her cage. It was at this time that Celine one day witnessed the sharing of one of these carrots, with Pookie nibbling at one end and her new, wild friend nibbling at the other end of the carrot, both inside the cage. The wild rabbits were somewhat scrawny and could easily pass through the wire mesh of the cage. My thoughts on the event were that word in the rabbit world had gotten around that our place was where, judging from Pookie's size, the living was good for rabbits. Later the wild rabbits vanished as suddenly and mysteriously as they had arrived.

Celine fed Pookie freshly pulled grass and dandelions from the lawn. On Pookie's birthdays, she decorated the sunroom with freshly cut garden veggies and created a "Happy Birthday, Pookie" sign hung on the wall between the sunroom windows. Delicious treats and fresh carrots with leafy tops were consistently supplied on Pookie's birthday parties. Celine and her friends she invited to the party would sang happy birthday songs to Pookie and had a blast with her. Pookie was truly adored by everyone. Neighbors would often bring their guests over, not to chat with us, but to visit with Pookie.

When Dad joined us, Pookie had already become a beloved member of the family. One of Dad's responsibilities was to feed her during the days when no one else was home. He started out his Pookie duty by following my rabbit care instructions one morning before I left home for work. "Place fresh hay and carrots in Pookie's cage. Don't forget to make sure Pookie has fresh water in her water bottle. She needs to drink lots of water, especially during hot weather," I reiterated. "Please don't forget to add carrot tops and Italian parsley; Pookie loves them," I said. Dad gazed at me silently, as if he were listening to a foreign language. "Don't forget to feed Pookie three times a day, Dad," I went on. "I usually feed her at 7:30 in the morning, then lunch, around noon; 5:00 PM is her supper time. Due to the large amounts of roughage in their diets, rabbits spend a lot of time eating. Don't forget to add two yogurt treats to her breakfast. Pookie loves those yogurt treats." My mind searched hard; I didn't want to leave any feeding details behind in the chambers of my brain. Dad finally broke his silence and said, with an obvious lack of empathy for our furry friend, "I know, I know. But, she's just a bunny rabbit." "Careful, you wouldn't want her to hear you talk like that," I admonished with notes of sarcasm, but also out of concern that Dad wouldn't exactly follow my instructions.

Terry and I planned another family camping trip, this time to the California Sierra in our comfy tent trailer. Dad refused to come along and agreed to look after Pookie while we were away. A few days before the trip, Dad and I went for a walk. I was hoping to change his mind during the walk, so found myself asking him the same question again.

"Are you sure you don't want to go with us?"

"I am not going camping." Dad was determined.

"I will make sure that you have enough food in the refrigerator."

"I don't need much."

"I will leave you Judy's, Lai-ying's, and Yi Yen's phone numbers, in case you need any Chinese groceries from over the hill." These were Chinese American friends that Dad had already met and felt comfortable with. "They could drive you to the Asian market there."

"I don't need anything, but I would like to go over the hill if they happen to go there," Dad seemed to be pleased with the idea of going to the Asian market.

"I will leave your doctor's name and phone number with the neighbor, in case you need any medical assistance while we are gone."

"Nothing will happen to me. But that's a good idea."

"Oh, and don't forget about Pookie. You'll need to feed her three times a day. I will make sure she has plenty of food and vegetables in the fridge before we leave. Don't forget about checking Pookie's water bottle," I said rather repetitively, still concerned about Dad's commitment regarding Pookie's welfare.

"You are more concerned about Pookie than me," Dad said firmly without showing any emotion on his face.

Was Dad joking? He can't be serious, I thought. His response to my requests was unexpected. I was astonished. For a while I didn't know how to react to his remarks. I slowed down my pace, stood on the road side for a few seconds, then said,

"Dad, why do you compare yourself with Pookie? She is a rabbit."

With a small grin Dad said, "Let's keep walking."

Pookie and Cooper have changed my attitude towards the well-being of any member of the kingdom Animalia in general. My sensitive side has come out. I am now more attentive to hearing often debated and complicated animal rights issues. I watch more movies about animals and pay more attention to literature regarding prevention of suffering and cruelty to animals. My heart hurts if I hear a story about injustice to the species that I love. The revolutionary thought of turning into a vegetarian has come to my mind frequently. For now I occasionally eat organic meat and love sea food. I consume lots of vegetables without thinking about killing any member of the kingdom Plantae. I am trying to be a better human being and to coexist in harmony with other species in nature.

Dad, on the other hand, was already a vegetarian. However, he has never given me a straight answer about his reason for avoiding any and all meat products. I don't believe he has ever consciously followed any worldwide debate on animal right issues, nor do I believe his decision to be a vegetarian had anything to do with love of dogs, cats, rabbits, and the like. His decision certainly wasn't a political one. It wasn't a "Chinese thing" to be concerned with issues such as animal rights back then. Naturally friends and family members had long ago accepted the fact that Dad was different. Deep down, many felt he was strange, since being a vegetarian was unheard of in our family circle. One time Dad's colleague persuaded him to eat a piece of pork sausage at a party. The colleague thought it was only a matter of trying. If Dad ate it, he would learn to like it and eventually become normal. The crowd at the party also encouraged him to try. Braving his soul, Dad caved in to peer pressure and swallowed the morsel and immediately threw up everything he had just had eaten. After the party, Dad was sick for a few days. Over the years, this horrible story has passed through my ears many times. If I asked for an explanation, Dad simply said to me, "I don't like the taste."

Dad's remarks reminded me of an experience that I had encountered when I paid my parents a visit in Beijing many years ago after I came to America. During the visit I met with a friend, a visiting scholar from China at the University of Nebraska at the time. He happened to be in Beijing when I was there on vacation. We decided to have lunch together at a well-known Korean restaurant on the west side of Xi Dan, one of the busiest streets in Beijing. Married to a Korean, my friend seemed to know every selection featured on the menu. He suggested that I try out his favorite cold noodle dish on the menu, one that had a simple description. The presentation of bowl of cold noodles in front of me seemed to be very "iron chef" style. The smell, the color of the noodle liquid, and few pieces of meat on top seemed especially fresh and appealing. The taste of the noodle threads was delicious! The texture of the meat, however, seemed to be different from the norm, once I surveyed it closely. "What a kind of meat is it?" I asked my friend cautiously before touching it. "Oh, just dog meat." Horrified, I felt an immediate forceful expulsion of the food in my stomach through my mouth; I was nauseated and wanted to throw up. In my youth I heard that Koreans eat dog meat but paid no attention to the gossip among the elders. My parents also told me that I once tried rabbit meat when I was a child, but I have no recollection of this either. Anyhow, I didn't believe my ears when my friend told me what was in my bowl that day. I was surprised that dog meat could still be served in Korean restaurants under the nose of the central government in the capital of China. Disgusted, I passed the entire bowl of Korean cold noodles to the friend. While I was sitting there staring at the meat I had just given away, the friend took great delight and wolfed down my bowl with gusto. I could never order any food from that restaurant ever again.

This event happened long before Cooper became my friend, long before Pookie joined the family, and long before I learned about the theory of coexistence, including care for animals and being compassionate towards all living organisms. Human compassion can be sustained through deep feelings of love for other species. I can never control how other people act, think, or what they put on their dinner table. One thing is for sure though: my love for Pookie and Cooper is real. I can never think of approaching any *Canis* or *Leporidae* meat ever again.

7. Money Tree

A huge skylight was installed in our home office before it was converted into a bedroom for Dad. The skylight brightened up the room during the day and invited the moonlight, the twinkling stars, and waving redwood branches to dance through at night. Dad could enjoy the magical sky at night while lying in bed. I decorated the bedroom with many memorable pictures, including a black and white one that I am especially fond of, which was taken of my parents together. In the picture Dad is unrecognizably slim while Mom is young and beautiful. One thing in common, looking seriously, both are wearing a dark Mao suit, "a combination of Chinese aesthetic taste and formality". A portable electric heater near Dad's bed made the room warm and cozy when the temperature was still cool outside and inside the house in early spring. A massage chair, foot rest, and a new 19" flat panel TV monitor had turned Dad into a couch potato. Our house is about seventy miles away from San Francisco where the Channel 26 studios are located. Channel 26 provides the local Chinese community with various Chinese language programs including domestic news, as well as news from China, Taiwan and Hong Kong. Dad had a structured daily schedule, as he pointed out to me once. The 8:00 AM news from China and Taiwan was a must-see. Glued to his chair, he never tired of watching the same news re-runs at lunch hour. At night, the time slot from 8:00 PM to 11:30 PM was a heaven for Dad. He could watch a variety of Chinese dramas as well as domestic news in Chinese. In between his TV shows, Dad would easily kill time by reading books about famous Chinese Red Army figures or personalities, as he mentioned to me. He was so familiar with these characters and had even marched with a few during the Anti-Japanese War and Chinese Civil War. His walks that I insisted on were about the only exercise he performed. Twice a day, Dad went for a walk by himself in the neighborhood, in the mornings and after supper with me.

Once called a third world country, China in just two short decades has become one of the most influential global powerhouses. Although the actual size of China's economy is debatable among economists, some say it is the second largest economy, next to the U.S. The recent Chinese economic reform has improved the living standard for everyone, especially for people who live in bigger cities. Joining Shanghai and Hong Kong, Beijing has become a city that houses the richest people in the country. People have money to spend and they know how to spend it. At the same time, the reform produced a big gap between the rich, in large cities, and the poor, scattered across rural China. The middle class has become more materialistic and has developed into one of celebrity worshipers. In order to catch up with the Joneses, the demand for better goods is spiraling up, higher than ever. People are openly seeking "the good life." Although wages for the work force have increased in recent years, there is a shortage of pension funds for retirees. China's entire retirement system needs to be reformed. Dad is one of those retirees who has not yet received a regular, annual adjustment to his pensions. Meanwhile, wages for the work force have kept increasing. Dad is unfortunately situated in the part of society that represents an enormous financial burden with its rapidly aging population.

Being a daughter, I have a duty to provide Dad with a better life. It is in my culture and so deep that I fear that it is in my genes also. This is a Chinese tradition; children, especially daughters of the family, should take care of their parents. Another tradition deeply rooted in the Chinese culture is gift-giving. The pressure of supplying gifts for Dad, our relatives, and family friends in Beijing was extremely high. Each time before Dad paid a visit to Beijing, he would spend considerable time in the States gathering gifts for them or items for himself. He would carefully clip ads from the Chinese newspaper that I subscribed for him. He also discovered the Quality Value and Convenience Channel (QVC) that became his favorite show on Saturday and Sunday mornings. Using the channel as his buying guide, Dad was constantly searching for new products he wished to purchase. However, his desire for new goods outstripped the number of dollars in his pocketbook. Balancing his budget suddenly became a serious issue.

One day, as I was passing by Dad's open bedroom door, I noticed a saleswoman on QVC demonstrating a chopper to her potential buyers. Pointing to the TV screen, Dad got excited.

"That chopper looks very useful," he said to me while staring at the monitor in amazement.

"Are you interested?"

"Yes, I'd like to take one back to Beijing."

"You don't even cook much in China. What would you do with it?"

"Oh, I'd like to cook for myself sometimes."

For the next few weeks, Dad and I were on a mission to find a suitable chopper at a bargain basement price. At first we thought it was *Mission Impossible*, good product, cheaper price than the ones sold on QVC? After investigating several local stores, we eventually bought one at the local Ross Dress For Less. Mission accomplished.

There are unwritten rules surrounding what is acceptable and what isn't when it comes to giving gifts to your friends and family members in China. However, those rules and the accepted code of buying and giving have become murky and foggy in my mind now after being in the States for so long. In the earlier years, when China was very poor, gifts, especially from the west, were appreciated. Nowadays China produces and imports almost anything imaginable. Ironically, presents bought in the States that you will take back to China are mostly made in China. Keeping face is a very important concept in Chinese society. You must show appropriate respect to the key family members and make sure you buy big name brand gifts for them instead of buying generic or lesser-known brands, otherwise you would lose face.

After several months of staying with me in the States, Dad planned another visit to Beijing. He had prepared a wish list for me, a list of gifts that he would like to take back, including items for him, my brother, my sister-in-law, his grandson, and other family friends.

The list included the following:

A box of non-stick pots and pans

A set of forks and knifes

A digital high resolution camera

A movie camera

A DVD player

An electric shaver

Several watches

Several pairs of shoes

A couple of handbags

Cosmetic jewelry

Make-up

Perfume

Tanning lotion (Samples for his grandson's new tanning business in Beijing)

Clothes

We went on a shopping spree and met our targets. Dad finally felt satisfied and was ready to leave.

China has transformed into a modern society in recent decades. Dad has also changed his tune within China's transformation. In many ways he doesn't seem to be the same person that I had always pictured him to be in my youth. Ever since he had been in the States, my frustration grew stronger as Dad's wish lists of gifts grew longer each year. With these wish lists and no source of money, I, the good daughter, became his financial supporter. I felt obligated to pay anything that he wished for. My memory of being a good daughter could be traced back to many years ago in Beijing. After receiving my first paycheck from my first teaching job, I gave it all to my parents. I was so proud that I was no longer a taker, but a contributor to the family. Months after that I continued giving, but my parents didn't want to accept any extra cash from me. Yet I insisted, so they continued accepting my earnings for a while.

Years later as a student in the U.S., still a good daughter, I saved every penny from my cafeteria job on an American university campus and spent most of it in Hong Kong on my way back to visit my parents in Beijing in 1984. It was trendy then to purchase and bring expensive electronic items back to China from overseas. There was an arrangement whereby I could purchase large household items outside China and have them shipped to my parents' home relatively inexpensively. I didn't want to be left behind or lose face, and so I joined the popular trend. In Hong Kong I bought a TV for my parents who couldn't afford a new one. The one that they were using at the time was still the one I gave to them in the late 1970s. I had won it in a lottery at my work place.

I also bought them a refrigerator, which they had never had before I left for America in 1981. For fear that the leftovers would go bad the next day, my parents often encouraged me to stuff myself at the dinner table. "Let's try to eat it up. Let's not even leave a single grain of rice on our plate," Mom said to me. "You are lucky to have food. Think about the poor kids in Africa who don't have anything to eat," noted Dad. Their suggestions tended to appeal to my conscience with some suggestion of guilt that if I didn't eat every last morsel, we'd all get sick the next day from botulism. I also had trouble understanding what my leftover rice had to do with starving kids in Africa, since it's not as if we could have sent the remainders overseas. After dinner I usually felt miserable for a couple of hours as my stomach ballooned out and tried to digest more helpings than necessary for my nutritional well being.

I also bought them an automatic clothes washer. They had never seen one in real life and always used to hand wash our clothes during my childhood years. Finding time to wash clothes was very difficult. Dad and Mom had to work six days a week, as did most of their generation. Sunday, the only day off in a week, was the date reserved for the household chores. I had a total of two outfits at any one point in time during my entire juvenile years. I normally wore one set for seven days, then changed to another set at the beginning of the next week. Thus, our clothes had to be hand washed on time, otherwise I wouldn't have any clean clothes for the next week. If my shirt or pants had holes, which happened often, Mom had to find extra time to patch the holes. Therefore there was a lot of pressure to get our clothes washed every Sunday.

Winter in Beijing was bitterly cold. I bought a wool sweater for Mom who didn't have the money to buy one made from genuine wool. Anything genuine was considered to be better than imitation or artificial. Summer weather in Beijing was hot and stuffy. No one in Dad's neighborhood of private homes had air conditioning. Even if one could afford an air conditioner, the electric bill could be exorbitant. So, on my 1984 return visit I bought my parents a portable fan made in Japan. Somehow I had the impression that the Japanese made the best fans in the world. "Japanese fans never stop working," Dad had remarked, as if he had owned one for many years. Indeed, this portable fan brought in Hong Kong decades ago is still in use and sits in Dad's living-room even today.

I also bought an Omega watch for Dad, who could never afford one again after losing his because of me. I have no idea how he got his first Omega, but Dad's story about it goes like this: As a child, I wasn't physically strong and got sick often. It cost very little to hire someone from the countryside to take care of me. Although my parents didn't have much, they needed someone to watch me. They hired a nanny from a small village nearby. The agreement was to pay no wages, but to provide her with room and board. She was willing to work, and life in the city was much better than living in her village. One time when I was very sick, Dad and the nanny rushed me to the hospital. Once they got there, Dad passed me to the nanny, told her to hold me and wait for him while he went looking for the doctor's office. But I started crying my lungs out and wouldn't let him go. He took his Omega from his wrist and let me play with it. I stopped screaming. By the time Dad had returned, his Omega had disappeared. I was too young to know what had happened to the watch. The nanny said to Dad she had nothing to do with the loss. In spite of a few clues that showed up later, Dad didn't want to blame the nanny. Ever since I heard the story, I was determined that I would buy Dad an Omega someday.

I felt so proud on the day when all my purchases were shipped from Hong Kong to my parents' house. These gifts for them came from the bottom of my heart. "You don't have to buy them for us. Life isn't easy in America," Dad said to me empathetically. Their living condition in China was poor and I just wanted to be responsible and be a good daughter, I thought. After my visit I continued to send them money on a regular basis. Dad told me on the phone, "We don't need it. Save it for yourself."

As time went by, people's attitudes about financial gain and commercial goods had changed significantly in China. Dad joined the crowd. The notion that all westerners were rich beyond belief quickly spread in Chinese society, especially among the young. I suddenly became wealthy simply because I was an American. A memory of buying an expensive camera sticks in my mind and still troubles me when thinking about it. It wasn't just an ordinary camera; it was a professional one that my parents insisted on and persuaded me to buy for my brother. It cost me over one thousand dollars to get the professional Nikon camera for someone who was an amateur. The professional magazine reviews reported that a lesser-known Pentax was a better buy, and as good or even better quality, but for my brother it had to be the big name brand or nothing. The cost didn't seem to be an issue to them. No questions were asked. It was a huge expense, costing me an arm and a leg, especially considering I had only just begun my new job after graduation. I unwillingly bought the camera anyway because I wanted to be a good daughter and a good sister.

I suppose one has to be very tolerant to marry into an interracial family. Terry has never complained much about the gift giving habits, nor does he stop me from buying anything that Dad wishes for. The word "No" isn't in my vocabulary when dealing with Dad's spending. I feel guilty that I have placed too much of a burden on Terry's shoulders. As a "foreign ghost", he is able to endure and has an ability to blend into this bowl of Chinese noodles well. I wonder if his sensitivity to a different culture comes from traveling around world. As a world traveler to the European continent, China, and Japan, Terry has also visited Turkey, India, Afghanistan, Pakistan, and Iran. He taught English as a second language in Taiwan between his college years. He has experienced different cultures and has witnessed poverty in the developing countries first hand. Perhaps all of the above doesn't relate to his tolerance and patience. Some people are born into the world with sensitive genes in their DNA. If that is the case, Terry is one of them.

I continued sending a monthly check to Dad, as long as he needed to pay the hospital bills for Mom. It was supposed to be a temporary arrangement but became a non-stop contribution even after Mom's passing away. Financially it was a stretch, nevertheless I felt obligated. A Chinese friend of mine once told me that he didn't want to visit China again. Each time he went his relatives asked him for money and gifts. The visits became too expensive for him to bear. At the time I wasn't quite convinced by his story. Now I understood what he meant. You were perceived to be well-to-do if you were from America or overseas. You would obviously have to give. People in China lived in decades of hardships and life struggles and had gone through many natural disasters and political turmoil in the past. Only in recent years could they afford to buy their first homes and cars, while in the States, ordinary citizens can easily get a loan to buy a house and own a car. On the surface Americans seem to have it all and live the American Dream. I often wonder if Dad truly comprehends that the houses and cars that most Americans have are not really theirs. The banks and mortgage companies are the true property owners. The so-called ordinary property owners still have to pay off the loans that they owe to the banks. The living standard is high in America, but people have lots of bills to pay. I am not quite sure if my relatives and friends in China understand that beneath the circumstances there are many subtleties involved. The popular notion of "yours is mine and mine is yours" has been rooted deeply in family units in Chinese society for thousand years and is still alive. This notion has left me rubbing my head with frustration.

Without exception, it is always my duty to give, regardless how I feel and what my financial circumstances are. I was a good daughter, as Dad reminded me many times. One day Dad was reading his Chinese newspaper in the bedroom. In it there was an article about an elderly disabled man who hadn't received any financial support from his children for a while. Dad called it to my attention across the hallway. "Look at this!" He pointed to the article's headline in displeasure. His face turned red with anger and I sensed his strong disapproval of the immoral behavior of the old man's children. At that very moment, I wondered if this was Dad's way of hinting to me that he didn't want to be in a similar situation as the old man. The effect of that newspaper story was profound. It was still in my mind as Dad and I were slowly pacing through the neighborhood woods that day. Silence permeated the air. I couldn't hear a bird singing or a sound of a squirrel scrambling on the tree branches nearby. I broke the silence and said to Dad,

"Why do you have to buy so many gifts?"

"I don't know what to do. So many people have expectations. Your brother and his wife took me out for dinner the day before I left China. And his adopted daughter invited me for lunch two days before that," Dad explained.

"Presenting gifts to other people should come from your heart. You shouldn't be forced to give," I said hoping to kill two birds with one stone. There was an instant silence and no response from Dad, who was walking slowly while gazing at the redwood trees on the side of the road.

"Life in America isn't as easy for me as it seems. I have worked so hard to get to this point," I went on. "Terry and I were poor students for a long time. Yes, we bought a house, but we still don't own the house, and have lots of bills to pay. We need to save some money for Celine's education. It is so expensive to send a child to a college in this country," I explained.

As I was talking to Dad, it occurred to me that as a child my parents didn't have to save up any money for my education, since schools in China were free at that time. Schools during the Cultural Revolution were closed and re-opened again when Deng came into a power in the early 1970s. Did Dad really understand what I was trying to tell him? I seem to have a comfortable life in America, but I am just middle class. The middle class in America nowadays means a struggling class.

"I am getting old. I need them to help me sometimes," Dad finally broke the silence.

"You can't buy help."

"It is the face thing, you know. I don't want lose face," Dad said simply.

"I am not a money tree. I have a family to take care of, Dad."

Dad refused to engage in any more dialogue on this topic with me after that. The walk that day was the most awkward time that we spent together as far as I could remember.

It was time for Dad to leave again; he planned it that way. About every six months, Dad felt the need to visit my brother and his grandson in Beijing for several months. As usual, a week before his departure Dad and I went to the bank. I secured some traveler's checks for him to use while he was in Beijing. Without counting the amount, Dad happily put them in his pocket and we then left the bank. Around about 10:00 PM that night, Dad called me to his room. "Wei," he said. "You only gave me six hundred dollars. It was always eight hundred dollars in the past," he went on with a long face. I was utterly numbed and couldn't utter a sound. My entire body was frozen still for a second. Then suddenly my blood floated again sending hot waves from my head to my toes. I felt my face warm. It turned hot and very red this time. Sorrow came over me and another wave of apprehension assailed me. I wanted to cry out, but my eyes were dry. My tears flooded inward gushing down into my heart. Instead of screaming, I muttered calmly, "I am sorry, Dad. I forgot that I gave you eight hundred dollars last time. I will get you more tomorrow." In a deep hole, I felt I couldn't get out. I had no guts to say no to Dad. There was so much pressure to give; where was the end? A sense of guilt took over my brain again. I shouldn't even think about an ending as long as Dad was alive. My parents gave birth to me and raised me. I felt a pang of shame to think Dad as my burden. But I am not a money tree, am I?

8. Childbirth

Dad is an orphan. I didn't find out about what really had happened to my grandpa until the Cultural Revolution started. During the revolution, since Dad was criticized for being a capitalist by the Red Guards, he wasn't trusted by the Communist Party that he had fought for, and consequently lost his position. The circumstances surrounding my grandpa's death suddenly became an issue held against Dad during the revolution. The Red Guards questioned Dad repeatedly and used "irregularities" in the story of Grandpa's death to interrogate him.

Dad has four uncles. His dad, my grandpa, the second son in the family, was very talented and well educated. According to Dad, Grandpa's mysterious death was connected with the political turmoil in China. In the early 1940s, Dad's uncle, the oldest in the family, was a college professor in Beijing (then called Peking), then controlled by the Nationalists. He had graduated from Qinghua University, a well-known institute in the country. Although he was far away from the rural village, the oldest uncle was a popular figure in the local area. At one point he was running for a senate seat in Peking and ended up losing the race because he couldn't raise enough money for his campaign.

Due to the political turbulence in the country at that time, the local postal service was often interrupted and sending or receiving letters from the Peking uncle was sometimes impossible. On top of that, most family members in the village were illiterate; the burden of drafting family letters to the uncle fell upon Grandpa who was a schoolteacher, and could also write Chinese calligraphy beautifully. Logically he was the messenger for the entire family in the village. In 1936 Mao set up his headquarters at Yan'an in the Shanbei region of Shaanxi province in China. From the late 1930s to the late 1940s, much of the countryside in the province, and in the rural areas of Shanxi province, Shaanxi's neighbor to the east, became important bases for Mao and his Red Army in the ensuing Chinese Civil War. There was a political movement initiated by the Communist Party at the liberated village of Wei Jia Tan in Shanxi Province at the beginning of the 40s. You could be in danger if you had any relatives associated with the party enemy, or lived in regions controlled by the Nationalists. You could be accused of being a rightist, a trader, or a spy by any members in the Communist Party. The local party members had, for a while, suspected Grandpa, since he had a close tie with and consistently contacted the Peking uncle on behalf of the family. They smelled a rat. In their eyes, Grandpa must have been an informer for the Nationalists.

Always on foot, Grandpa went to work at the school during the day and came back home at night. Although his school was miles away from the village, the trek was his daily routine, rain or shine. But abruptly one day Grandpa didn't return home. He didn't show up for two weeks and no one knew where he was. The family was deeply concerned and, at the same time, had heard that the party was investigating anyone who had had a connection with the Nationalists.

Eventually the news broke: the family received a report that Grandpa had been arrested by the local party members. Not until several years later did Dad learn that my grandpa was forced to report to the party in writing what he had learned about from the Peking uncle and about his special ties to the Nationalists. Grandpa refused to answer the questions and for that he was sent to the local prison.

A few weeks after his interrogation, Grandpa died. Soon after Grandpa's passing, the party representative told the family to claim the body. Dad was too young to understand anything at the time. His third uncle took him to see the body that was still in the prison cell. When they got there, a guard, sullen and completely unsympathetic, unlocked the cell and let them in. It was small and gloomy without any windows. On the right side of it there was a simple and narrow bed where Grandpa's body lay. In the corner, on the other side of the cell, there was a big ceramic pot. In the old days, the locals stored their well water in big ceramic pots. They later used them for drinking, cooking, and washing. No chairs, table, or other furniture were there. The guard told them that Grandpa killed himself. At the time he was found dead, the guards said that his head was down in the ceramic pot and his body was leaning against it. But Dad's third uncle didn't believe the story. He insisted Grandpa died in the hands of the party members. Bruises and wounds suspiciously covered Grandpa's body. These circumstances did not point towards suicide. Undoubtedly he had been beaten and tortured. At the time of his death, Grandpa was only in his thirties. The family laid him to rest in the family plot at the village cemetery where my grandma had also been buried years earlier. That was the saddest day in Dad's life, he later told me. At the age of seven, Dad became an orphan.

As a child I learned that my grandma died in childbirth. It was an open secret; everyone in the family knew it, yet Dad had never discussed it. I suppose it was too painful for him to revisit. My curiosity about Grandma's death had increased once I became a mother. Before giving birth to Celine, the word childbirth had tormented me for years and given me goose bumps whenever I thought about it. Being aware of Grandma's tragedy and hearing the painful firsthand childbirth stories told by my friends in Beijing, and even the sound of the word "childbirth", I had come to associate it with suffering, pain, and death. At one point I was so sure I was never going to give birth to a child because I simply couldn't bear the pain. The tables were turned and by the time I reached forty I was well aware of my biological clock ticking. I had changed my mind. After two years of trying, tons of pills, frustrations, and floods of tears, the result was empty handed at the end of a long difficult process. Just as I was about to give it up, to my surprise, bingo, I was pregnant after ten years of marriage. Now I would have to face reality and actually give a birth to a child.

Natural childbirth is extremely popular in the community where I now live. When it is time to deliver a baby, some women, shunning the available hospital facilities, invite a mid-wife to their homes. A friend of mine did just that and even video taped the event so that she could proudly show it to her friends at get-togethers. Being pregnant, I had an opportunity to attend birth workshops provided by the local hospital. These workshops were designed for couples, but also intended to help women to overcome their fear of painful birth. My goal of attending was simple: I wanted to find out what my options were and what medical interventions my doctors could offer to relieve my physical and psychological pain when my time came.

During a brief search I bumped into two books, *Natural Childbirth* and *Childbirth Without Fear* by Grantly Dick-Read (January 26, 1890 – June 11, 1959), a British obstetrician who believed that "women who are adequately prepared are innately able to give birth to their child, without external intervention." Childbirth without fear? A dread took root in the deep hollow of my heart upon hearing the word "fear". I remember at one of my birth workshops I was asked to imagine a landscape with beautiful flowers and green grass while learning the breathing techniques. The breathing techniques didn't seem to work for me no matter how hard I tried. With my eyes closed I couldn't see any beautiful imaginary landscapes in my mind. All I could imagine at that moment was the painful labor that I was about to experience in a few months.

"This won't work for me," I said anxiously to Terry, who was sitting by my side on the floor during one of the series of classes.

"Why don't you try it one more time," he said encouragingly.

"I give up. I can't learn how to be natural," I responded with certainty.

I respect the women who bravely face their fear and prepare to give birth without any medical interventions. I admire those who are into the natural movement. Those women are strong, brave, and empowered by their faith in the theory of natural birth. I, on the contrary, am a coward.

Terry and I were very excited to find out that we were going to have a baby girl – our siblings were all brothers. In preparing to give birth to our daughter, I wondered about the theory of natural birth that I had read about. Studies suggested that historically women gave birth at home without medical interventions, often under risky circumstances and an unclean environment. These births were generally attended by a midwife or members of the birthing woman's family. Later external interventions were introduced and the conventional assumptions associated with childbirth were challenged. For mothers who adopted medical intervention techniques, mortality rates for both mothers and their babies were exceptionally low. However, by the beginning of 1940s, some medical professionals started questioning the safety of such external intervention. As a result, several medical professionals and midwives, such as Michel Odent, Frederick Leboyer, and Ina May Gaskin, pioneered "birthing centers, water birth, and safe home birth" as alternative places and methods to the hospital model. While some women have now embraced these pain management techniques during natural childbirth, others consider it to be primitive and to cause unnecessary suffering. Many women feel less stress and anxiety surrounding the birthing process when they know that medical interventions and pain relief will be available. I have to admit that I am one of those women who feel the need for a medical intervention. I am neither a medical professional nor an expert on any childbirth issues, and have no desire to engage in further discussions on natural birth versus external interventions. I deeply respect any women who choose a different path. I can only say how I feel from my own childbirth experience.

My bleeding started at 12:00 AM. It was early Halloween morning and ghostly dark outside. I woke up Terry from his deep dreams. His eyes were barely open but he rolled up from the bed, quickly threw on some clothes, grabbed a jacket and the car keys, and rushed me to the local hospital. The streets were empty and still dark with the dim light from a half moon hanging in the sky. Kids and ghosts were still sleeping.

When we arrived I was immediately admitted into the hospital room to wait for my labor. The wait was long. My contractions hadn't yet started, but my anxiety and anticipated labor pain were strong and unbearable. By late afternoon, when most kids started trick or treating on the streets, my water broke in the hospital room. Lying on the bed, I felt mild contraction pains. Suddenly a loud scream from the room next door pierced the silence. It was a cry from a woman who seemed to exhaust all her strength and pleaded for relief and escape from her birth pains. Her painful cries penetrated the thin walls and sent shivers down my spine. I had never heard any cries like these from a human being before. They sounded as if the woman was being tortured and about to be executed. The effect of the waves of screams had a greater impact on me. Trembling and shocked, I turned around and looked at Terry, who was staying with me, and said to the nurse, "Give me the epidural now!" As expected, the epidural worked wonders for me. The rest of the time I was able to feel the contractions and had no pain during my intensive labor. After about twenty minutes of pushing, I gave safe birth to an alert and healthy baby girl in the early morning after the long Halloween night. Although it would have been interesting to have a child with a birthday on Halloween, I was relieved that my daughter had been born the day after, which I considered a more auspicious day to celebrate a birthday.

As a mother, I often thought about my grandma's mysterious death. My chances of finding out about this mystery became possible once Dad joined me in the States. Finally one day in the spring of 2006 during our daily walk, I felt right and built up my courage. "Dad, I know Grandma died of childbirth. Could you tell me what exactly happened to her?" I asked nervously. A cloud passed over Dad's face. Staring at the road ahead, Dad kept walking slowly and silently for a minute. It seemed he was trying to get his thoughts together. I wondered if I had just broken open a wound. Dad raised his head and gazed at the distant crown of a redwood tree that towered by the road side a few yards away. Taking a deep breath, he simply said, calmly and softly, "My mom passed away before she was thirty. I am the oldest child. My mom died when she was giving birth to her second child."

Thoughts flooded my brain as Dad was talking. I wondered if Dad could really recall any details involved in her death. Dad was only five when Grandma died. I wondered how a tragic event such as this would affect one's life. I wanted to dig further. I wanted to learn the real story from Dad.

"How did she die, do you remember?"

"Yes. I remember."

"What happened?"

"She was giving birth and had difficulties. She was scream-ing and crying loudly."

"Who was there to assist the childbirth? Did the family find a doctor or send her to a hospital?"

"We were in a poor rural area. The village had no doctor or a hospital nearby. Someone from the same village helped with her childbirth. It was a common practice in the area at that time."

"It must have been very hard for you to hear your mom screaming like that at such young age."

"Yes. I still hear her screams, whenever I think of her."

"What happened after that?"

Taking a deep breath, Dad said quietly, "The relatives didn't want me to hear more of her screams and cries, so they took me away. Later I was told that both my mom and the baby had died during the birth."

The neighborhood road that we were so used to seemed to be endless that night. There is an old Chinese saying, "Easy up, and difficult down," (*Shang shan rong yi, xia shan nan*). While it didn't seem to be easy while Dad and I climbed up to the top at the end of the road, it seemed to be even more difficult coming down. Our steps going down were hesitant and painfully slow. I had no more questions for Dad. I didn't know what to say next, nor did I know how to comfort his sorrow. Dad's memory of his mom's passing was a huge hole in an existing wound buried deep in his heart. The hole was too sensitive to be poked further. Dad and I paced down in low spirits without engaging in any more conversation. The sun began sinking gradually behind the redwood trees and the neighborhood houses. Soft white cotton balls of clouds were transitioning to a dark grey mass which was slowly enveloping the blue roof of the sky by the time we reached home.

The next day during our walk Dad told me that my grandpa later re-married. The woman he married was from a village thirty miles away. Dad referred to Grandpa's second wife as "the woman". He didn't know her real name, Dad said. She was introduced to Grandpa by an acquaintance in her village. "The woman" was previously married, but had no children. Her village was half way between Grandpa's school and his village. There was no convenient or formal mode of transportation. First Grandpa walked half way from the school to his second wife's village and refreshed himself there for a while. Then he had to keep on walking all the way home from her place. He did it a couple of times a week. Traveling on foot was common in those days since there was no other means of transportation. This journey was later simplified once "the woman" moved into Grandpa's house in his village.

Only one year after his second marriage, Grandpa passed away. Dad had no real relationship with the second wife; "the woman" soon moved out of the family house. "There was lots of sorrow in my heart. Imagine, my mother passed away and two years after that, my dad died. That was the darkest time in my life," Dad said painfully. The living situation in the village got worse once Dad lost both of his parents. Having learned about the news, his fourth uncle sent a letter to the family and asked if Dad would like to join him in Yan'an where the Red Army was based. Dad jumped at the opportunity and left the village for good. He was twelve years old.

Three women, Grandma, "the woman", and I, are from different generations. I can't imagine putting myself in Grandma's or "the woman's" shoes, nor can I picture myself living in the same condition that both women had lived. Perhaps Grandma would have survived childbirth if she were in today's medically advanced society. She would have had many choices and an array of tools to assist her to make right decisions for her own body and health. She could have been able to free herself from her birth pain and suffering by choosing medical interventions or various alternative birthing methods. Dad would still have had his mom, one of the most important figures in a child's life. The hollow at the base of Dad's heart could have been filled by unconditional love, joy, and nurturing from his mom. "The woman", who had never met or knew Grandpa before her arranged marriage, had to quickly adapt to life with a stranger. She then vanished soon after her second husband's death. Where did that poor woman go, I wondered? Did she remarry again? Living in a feudalist Chinese society, did she suffer discrimination by the local people for being married twice? Dad was too young to get to know "the woman". No one knew or had traced where she went. As an educated woman in a modern society, I have control of my body and soul; I have freedom of choice. Today I am able to make intelligent choices for myself by researching and gathering reliable information and learning from the experiences of friends and family. Perhaps the outcome of one's fate and destiny is in the hands of the society or cultural environment in which one lives. In an enlightened, civilized, and more technically advanced society, we have a tendency to lose our innocence. At the same time, we have gained more options, more opportunities, and freedom.

9. Little Emperor and Little Princess

Mao Mao with his grandparents

I was in the States when Mao Mao was born. Mao Mao literally means "hairy", and is not to be confused with Chairman

Mao. The name has nothing to do with Mao Mao being hairy either. It is a nickname sometimes given to a cute and cuddly Chinese baby boy. Mao Mao is my brother's son and the only grandson of my parents. "Beauty is in the eyes of the beholder." Dad often says proudly. "Everyone in our family has big eyes. My grandson has big eyes. His looks go with the family." Somehow having big eyes is important; they are a symbol of one's beauty, according to Dad. Most Chinese have narrow and small eyes. Does that make big-eyed people special? Dad thinks that is the case. It is a plus. Mao Mao also has fair skin. In China, fair skin seems to be nobler than the darker tones that many Chinese people have. I suppose that in China if you had darker skin you'd prefer to have lighter skin. Or, if you were too fair skinned, you would like to be darker. Many people in America go to tanning salons regularly or take a sunbath on beaches to get tanned. In their minds, darker toned skin seems healthier and more beautiful.

To Dad, Mao Mao was the most handsome, good-natured, and simply the best baby in the entire universe. The boy is everything to him. He is the future of our clan. Confucius, an ancient Chinese thinker and social philosopher, once said, "There are three ways of being disloyal to your ancestors. Not carrying on the family name is the worst." There is no doubt in Dad's mind: his grandson will carry on the family name to the next generation and generations to come. When he was young, Mao Mao had an ability to tease his grandpa, play with his hair, and sit on Grandpa's legs at any time, at any place, and still can get away with it and make Dad feel happy. Remarks from his grandpa towards such childish behaviors were often affectionate. "Nutty boy," Grandpa said to the boy, always with a huge cheerful grin. I caught Mao Mao in action a few times during my return visits. Dad enjoyed every minute of whatever the boy did to him. In his eyes

WEI WEI

Mao Mao could do no wrong. Certainly Mao Mao was born with great expectations. Under the one-child policy to limit China's population growth that was launched in the 1970s, the birth of Mao Mao was a very special event for Dad.

Mao Mao's parents were in their twenties when he was born. Financially, the young couple wasn't yet established. By offering a helping hand, my parents opened their wallet and home to the baby and hired a nanny to look after him during the day. At night and during the weekend, the little boy would go home with his parents. The boy was adored by everyone, especially by Dad, and was showered with hugs, kisses, and toys. The first time I met Mao Mao was in Beijing when I was on a vacation. Under instructions from Dad, I bought a gift for him – a remote control toy car – in the States before leaving. Mao Mao was two years old then. He loved the gift. Once the toy was in his hands, no one was allowed to touch it. Using the wireless remote control, he moved the toy car forward, backward, and ran it in all directions in the living room. Everyone was watching him with amusement. One day during my visit, the whole family took the boy to the People's Park in the city. The boy insisted on bringing the toy car with him. No one dared to say no to him. He drove the car as we walked through the park and spun it around and around in front of an adoring crowd. The crowd was laughing and clapping, especially Dad, who was his number one cheer leader. Mao Mao had a blast. He was the center of the attention, the apple of Dad's eye. He would bring great prosperity to our family.

One would think that young boys usually are oblivious about fashion trends, but Mao Mao loved clothes and shoes with well-known brand names. He had a desire to look better under his peer pressure. He went to well-known schools and was a good student up until his last high school year. Dad wanted Mao Mao to study law at Beijing University, which was the Chinese equivalent of Harvard University and Cambridge. Preparing for a college entrance exam in Beijing was mentally draining and extremely stressful. During his preparation for the all-important exam, Mao Mao's parents got divorced. The loving care from his grandparents couldn't deflect this devastating blow on the boy. The breakup affected Mao Mao emotionally and spiritually.

Only a small fraction of applicants can get into college in China. Due to the relatively small number of colleges, there is extreme competition to score well. There is a selection process in the national examination system for college admissions that is a prior requirement for entrance into almost all colleges and universities at the undergraduate level in China. In general, candidates list their university or college preferences in several tiers prior to the exam. Candidates for college are selected and then admitted by each college every year after entrance exams are over. Their admissions are solely based on their test scores. Even a small difference in grades can mean the difference between getting into a good university and a second tier institution. Unfortunately, Mao Mao scored two points short of meeting the standard for Beijing University. That was a huge disappointment for Dad. The dream of his grandson becoming a lawyer was slipping away in front of his eyes. The boy had to settle for less. He got into a second tier college in Beijing and was a student there for only a year. That college wasn't good enough; it wasn't the Beijing University that Dad hoped for. Somehow education systems overseas seemed to be superior, especially the ones in a western society. The family decided to send Mao Mao abroad to study.

Mao Mao ended up at Christchurch, "Garden City of the World", in New Zealand. He was a college student for three years and according to Dad, he had a harsh experience there. The boy wasn't used to the local cuisine and didn't know how to cook for himself. Such an unsatisfactory state of existence gave cause for concern. "He likes Chinese food. He doesn't eat well there," said Dad. "He doesn't like to associate with the New Zealanders. For the most part he only hangs out with his Chinese and Japanese friends," Dad went on. Mao Mao shared an apartment with two other Chinese students. One day, after they came back for the school, they found the apartment ransacked. One of his roommates had lost his TV set and a camera. The boys suspected that some natives had committed the crime. The incident convinced Mao Mao to believe that New Zealand wasn't a safe place to stay. He couldn't see a bright future ahead if stayed the course. Dad and his parents encouraged him to pursue a successful life overseas, but the boy stubbornly refused any advice from them. He eventually managed to get a business degree and a certificate for English as Second Language. "China is my future," he declared. Against all odds, Mao Mao packed it in and bought a one-way airline ticket back to Beijing. This was another huge disappointment for Dad.

I have only met Mao Mao a few times over his twenty-seven years of life. My sparse contact with him was indirect and mainly through Dad. In response to family wishes, I had sent Dad a few thousand dollars in total over the years to support the boy's education and his expensive habits. Traditionally boys were favored in China. Boys were supposed to look after property, inherit fortunes, and subsequently were favored with more opportunities to get ahead in life than girls. By the end of the Cultural Revolution, whether one could or could not get into the higher education system depended largely upon the luck of the draw when universities re-opened their doors to students right after Deng Xiao Ping took over the power. In this case, good luck fell upon me. Being the girl in the family, I often wonder whether I would have been less valued if I hadn't received a higher education in Beijing or in America. Dad would never admit that he had Confucian values. Confucian values were frequently attacked by the Chinese Communists, since they were considered as a cause of the "ethnocentric closed-mindedness". He wasn't supposed to have Confucian traditional values as a member of the Red Army. Ironically, I am considered the richest and the "iron rice bowl" by my family. In the eyes of my folks, I made it. Somehow the notion that I am well-to-do and successful is solely based on the fact that I live in America. Even though I have only spent limited time with Mao Mao, I am still regarded as the aunt and an influential close relative. I have an obligation to help to fulfill any of his wishes. I have learned that any questioning of Mao Mao's intentions or habits would result in an uncomfortable situation. That is the family tradition and an unwritten rule that I dare not break.

Tanning services were unheard of in China until fairly recently. In the spirit of budding entrepreneurial ventures nationwide, Mao Mao decided to open a tanning salon in Beijing upon returning. I suppose he got the idea from being in New Zealand. He also intended to purchase tanning lotions from the States for the new business. While Dad was with me in the States, we were always on the move during the weekends. We visited several local tanning services, collected various samples of tanning lotions from the local tanning stores, and shipped them to Beijing. Whatever the boy wanted, he got.

Setting up one's own business is a huge task, even for the experienced. Mao Mao had never owned a business before. Dad was concerned about his grandson's ability to take on such an adventurous project. Being an ocean apart from him, Dad nonetheless wanted to be hands-on. I purchased a calling card for him to call China often. The calling system was complicated and difficult to use since Dad didn't understand English. He created an easy system for himself. On a piece of paper, with my translation, Dad patiently wrote down detailed instructions in Chinese that the calling system had provided – the eight hundred number, the pin code, the country code, and the area code. He would carry the paper in his pocket wherever he went, ready to go into action for his grandson at any time. His mission often included visiting the local tanning services and investigating American tanning lotions, then he would report the findings back to the boy. The aggregate amount of time Dad had spent on the phone with his grandson was enormous and more than he did with his son. The boy's tanning enterprise finally opened for business in a part of Beijing frequented by foreign visitors. After only a few months, the business took off. It was one of the first two tanning services operated in the entire capital city. Meanwhile in the States, the news media and dermatologists had been issuing statements about the danger of frequently using tanning beds, which greatly increase a person's risk of developing skin cancer. These negative pronouncements, however, have had virtually no dampening effects on the boy's flourishing tanning business.

Nevertheless, Dad loves Mao Mao more than anyone else. His grandson was the shining star for the future. China's one child policy has produced many little Emperors. Mao Mao is certainly the Emperor of our clan.

Celine with her grandpa

A few weeks after Celine was born, I sent a photo of her to my parents. Mom had gone blind by this time. Dad got the picture, then hastily called from Beijing. "The baby has a big head. She doesn't look like anyone from our family." I suppose Terry wasn't included in the context of our family. There is an old saying in China, "Daughters are like water that splashes out of the family and cannot be recovered back after marriage." In recent years, the tide has turned. The trend of preference for boys has changed in big cities. Now many people have a preference for girls under the belief that girls are more likely to care for their elders. I'd like to think that Dad has no prejudice against girls.

Mom's health was rapidly declining. Time seemed to be running out for Celine to visit Grandma, even just once. By the time Celine had reached six months old in 1996, I took temporary leave from work and boarded a plane to China with her, leaving Terry behind as his job required. I always have a problem sleeping on planes; I am amazed that anyone can do it. A friend of mine told me that once she travelled from here to Iran by plane and slept all the way. By the time she woke up, she had already arrived. I suppose people like her are wired differently than me. Or perhaps they were the kind who belongs to a frequent flyers club that allows them to reserve specific seats, such as those with more leg room or adjacent to unoccupied seats for more leg room. Anyway, my flight to Beijing was long and uncomfortable. I was wide awake for the most part. However, luck struck again even though I had no upgrade on my ticket. The seat next to mine was empty! I was able to convert it to a perfect bed for the baby to sleep on.

Celine was a sleepless baby. If she happened to fall asleep, most likely it would only be a short nap. I wondered where she got that energy from. Certainly it wasn't from me. Was she hungry? Couldn't be; I had just breast fed her. I played with her for a while, walked up and down in the aisle with her in my arms, and had a few breaks in between. I was dog tired by the time we landed at the Beijing airport.

At the airport Dad greeted us warmly. I surveyed him for a minute, noticing that he had added some deep facial lines and had put on a few more pounds. This gain of weight came from uncontrollably eating sumptuous Chinese food, especially Chinese noodle dishes. He was too weak to resist such a temptation. In addition he refused to engage in any exercise that might have helped his constitution. Anyhow, Dad was very happy to see us. His face lit up and his eyes beamed with excitement. His mouth was wide open with a huge grin as soon as he spotted Celine who was asleep in her baby basket. He gazed at her face for a few seconds and said, "She doesn't look the same as she was in the photo you sent me after her birth." Did this mean Celine finally got a stamp of approval from Dad, I wondered? The noise and foot traffic at the luggage claim woke up the baby. Her choppy little face was white and delicate; her cheeks were pink; her big eyes were wide open, staring at the ceiling and at the strange faces around her. This beautiful child, lost in transition, couldn't figure out where she was and who these people were. At only six months old, how could she logically comprehend her present situation? Perhaps she was thinking she had just landed on a wonderland or on another planet. It was impossible for her to think all of that. Babies eat, cry, and sleep; adults don't really know what they are thinking. Although in her new book, *The Philosophical Baby*, Alison Gopnik, a psychologist, argues that babies are much smarter than we think, and in many ways more intelligent than grown-ups. I wondered if we are trying to guess at babies' thoughts in conjunction with their behaviors. I am sure that psychologists will one day truly discover for certain that babies can actually understand more than adults think they can. Celine muttered something that no one around her could understand in a language only babies knew. I suppose she was saying, "Very nice to meet you, Grandpa." Dad couldn't help smiling. "She looks like a member of our family. She has our DNA," he said proudly.

Spring in Beijing is hot, dry, and windy. The gusts of warm wind from Inner Mongolia often blow over, crossing the northern mountain ridges on the Mongolian plateau to the capital city, generating clouds of yellow dust and tinging the blue roof of the sky with a yellowish-brown. By June and July the temperature sometimes rises above 30 Celsius – almost hot enough to cook a pizza outside. We had an air conditioner inside the house, purchased as a gift to my parents a year ago. I planned to stay inside with Celine during the day. The cost of electricity in the capital was high and the air conditioning was working only part time at my parents' place that summer. Dad said to me, "it is not good to use it for a long time. Your mom can't stand the harsh cold air from the machine." They still kept the fan going, however, the one I bought for them ten years ago in Hong Kong. "The air from the fan is much softer and gentler – much better," Dad said. Thus, for the most part we were cooled by the gentle breeze of the fan, while the air conditioning unit stood idly by.

As Mom's main caregiver, Dad was as busy as a one-armed paper hanger. My cousin from her family's farm was looking for a job in the city that summer. In between her job hunting she occasionally provided a helping hand. Nevertheless, I was fully occupied with Celine. There were no carpets on the concrete floor in the house. Grandma's queen-sized bed became Celine's playpen where she spent most of her time during the day. Fearing that she might fall on the concrete floor, we had someone in the house sitting at the edge of the bed watching her continuously. For the most part Mom, who couldn't see and move freely but could hear where Celine ventured to, was the perfect security guard sitting there. The temperature inside the house got hotter in the afternoons. One of the common problems for babies is development of rashes on their bottoms if they aren't dried or cleaned. A simple solution to this problem is to have babies crawling around without diapers. Celine often played and crawled on her grandma's bed with a bare bottom. She would pee on the bed if not caught on time. "Did she pee on the bed again?" Grandma asked, reaching one hand to feel the bed sheet. No one wanted to tell her the truth. We simply responded, "No. It is dry." Mom was a clean fanatic. We often joked that she had a bit of OCD (obsessive-compulsive disorder). Every inch in the house had to be super neat and clean. When we touched anything in the house, no single dust particle was allowed to be found. If she knew what Celine did on her bed, she certainly wouldn't be pleased.

One memory of this time period in particular flashes across my mind. One time I heard a loud cry from Celine. I rushed to find that she had fallen to the floor from the bed near her playpen. Mom was sitting there helpless. Tears clouded my eyes and then went rushing down like a stream onto my cheeks. I picked her up quickly, holding her tight and gently stroking her little trembling body in my arms. Dad hurried to my site. "Why are you crying? She is all right," he said to me plainly. What Dad had just said left me feeling ashamed. Was I overly protective of my child? Being a first time Mom, did I exaggerate the situation? Or was I feeling sad because of Mom's current condition? Mom wasn't really here for her granddaughter, was she? She couldn't be a normal grandma to Celine, could she? In a way, Celine had already lost her grandma. I felt the earth giving way beneath me. My beloved Mom who was here with us didn't really seem to be here in the present.

By the end of September I was eager to return to America with Celine. I was glad we had visited Mom, but felt happy to leave. This turned out to be the only time that Celine was with her grandma in her lifetime. Mom wasn't able to see her granddaughter, but she could touch, kiss, and hold her. Dad phoned me soon after we returned. "Sorry I wasn't able to look after Celine when you were in Beijing. Your mom needs a lot of attention, you know," he apologized. Being over five thousand miles away, he regretted he wasn't able to be close to his granddaughter.

When Dad saw Celine at the San Francisco airport in February 2004, she was no longer a choppy baby; she was eight years old –a big girl. Based on Kimberly Keith's article, "Building Character - Child Development - The Eight-Year Old", this is the age when "social comparison becomes a basis of self-evaluation." Celine was very much into her Game Boy, wearing clothes from Limited Two, and was about ready to move on to Abercrombie Fitch and Forever 21 in just a few years. On the way home from the airport, Celine, looking bored, kept silent and was not able to understand any of the exciting discussions we were engaged in with Grandpa. Soon after we had supper that night, Dad dragged his suitcase to the living room floor. In it he retrieved several gifts that he had bought for Celine – a necklace, a pair of earrings, a ceramic bracelet, and a ring, all in a traditional Chinese design. Celine didn't know how to react to the costume jewelry that wasn't normally a part of her collection. What to do with them? She now had to think outside the box. At last Dad, from underneath his clothes in the suitcase, pulled out a doll dressed in traditional Chinese clothes. "Look. I have this for you," Dad said in Chinese to Celine with a huge grin. Celine reached out her hands greedily, grabbing the doll instantly. Her eyes were wide open but she couldn't utter a sound. "Did you say thank you?" I asked her. "Thank you, Grandpa," Celine muttered in English. She couldn't take her eyes away from her new doll that was so foreign, so different from all her Bratz and Babies. She put her new friend on display up on the top of her bedroom dresser. She didn't play with the doll ever again. Howeve, it became one of the items in her Chinese exhibition.

From Grandpa Celine learned to say "How are you?", "I am hungry," and "where is the bathroom?" in Chinese, then refused to engage in any more learning beyond these basics.

Grandpa, against his own promise, didn't try to learn English either. He hid his English lessons on tape brought from China in his bedroom closet, listened to them only once, and never bothered to listen to them again. Communication between Dad and Celine took place mostly in sign language. Celine didn't like Chinese food, especially her grandpa's cooking. On the days when Dad offered to cook dinner for us, something different had to be prepared for her. Her favorites were cheese burgers, macaroni, and pizza. To encourage a more intimate bond between grandpa and granddaughter, I took Dad along with me when picking up Celine after school. Together we also participated in open house and a few other memorable school events. It was my intention to provide Dad with a sample of Celine's daily life and her school system. A few events later, Dad politely declined an invitation. "I have seen enough. I prefer to stay at home tonight," he said.

Celine was home in between her summer camps from June to August. Dad kept an eye on her during the day when both Terry and I were at work. Lunch was a challenge. Celine didn't like Grandpa's steaming noodles. I stocked the refrigerator with weekly supplies of TV lunches. Celine occupied herself either by reading books or playing computer games in her room, while Grandpa was watching the Chinese news on TV. There was a break for Dad and Celine in late morning every day. In his younger years, Dad had played badminton quite well and was known to be sharp and fast on the court. While he was here we had played some informal matches. Not wanting to hurt my feelings, Dad would let me win. Although he was not as fast as his previous legs could carry him, he still had the skill. I knew if Dad didn't pretend to lose, I could never win a game. Grandpa showed Celine how to play badminton on our driveway in front of the garage during the break. The granddaughter was eager to learn the ropes from the old hand. Somehow they managed to communicate using their sign language. A few rounds into one match, Grandpa had to stop to catch his breath. The game was too much for his overweight body to endure.

Once in a while Celine was interested in walking with us after supper. Our narrow road unfortunately didn't have a sidewalk. One day, pushing her scooter on the road, she left Dad and I far behind. "Don't go too far. Watch for cars on the road," Dad shouted to her. Celine didn't understand a word of what Grandpa said. She continued charging ahead. "You have to teach Celine some Chinese," Dad said to me seriously. "Learning has to come within oneself. It can't be forced," I countered. To minimize the damage, I adjusted my tone and then assured Dad that someday Celine would be ready to learn, but it would have to originate on her own initiative. Dad's lecture about the importance of Chinese language followed and dominated our remaining conversation that night. As a parent I wasn't on the right track, according to Dad. Chinese, the language his granddaughter should learn and master, would be a great skill to have in contributing to her bright future.

My parents were affectionate people. A simple act of touching a shoulder or kissing my cheek would make me feel loved as a child. When sad or stressed without any reason, I always found comfort in their gentle acts and their expressions of love through words and touch. Their affections could magically calm me down and stop my tears. Dad's consoling arms around my shoulders could change stormy weather into sunshine. Such intimate behavior was a token of trust among us in the family, but seemed to be lost on Celine's generation. In a minimal touch modern American society, Grandpa's affection was new to Celine. He was one of the closest relatives in the family, yet was so foreign to his granddaughter. One stranger isn't supposed to be so affectionate to another. A stranger isn't supposed to trust another instantly. A few times Grandpa's touch on his granddaughter's back or shoulders was received negatively. Feeling awkward and rolling his eyes, Dad couldn't figure out what to make of Celine's rejections. His frozen smile conveyed his obvious hurt. Trust runs in a family, however, in this case the bond was too green to gain the kind of trust Dad had wished for. It takes a long time to build a solid foundation. Breaking cultural and communication barriers needs more effort, even within a family. During Dad's stay, the bond between Dad and Celine improved gradually over time. The level and the depth of their closeness still weren't fully developed, nor were they the same as Dad had towards his grandson, the little emperor, Mao Mao. Yet Celine remains his little foreign princess who is so close, yet so distant, like a tiny glow from afar under a shaft of sunlight.

10. Too White

Terry at Yosemite

My parents wanted to have a good talk with me in the family room a day before leaving for my adventure in America in 1981. The atmosphere in the room was sober and stifling. Dad and Mom were sitting on a sofa chair on each side of the coffee table. Soon after I settled down on a chair in front of them, they began with their dos and don'ts. They knew that once I was out of the house, especially being an ocean apart,

I would be out of their range of control. This was an opportunity for them to lecture me before sending me far away, much like getting a dose of protective flu shots before the flu season begins. I was sitting there listening quietly, just nodding "yes, yes". After lecturing me for a few minutes, they went silent. It seemed there was something on their minds, something they were struggling to say to me, yet they didn't know how to start. Mom gazed at me for a moment and out of the blue she said, "You are still young. In terms of marriage, we hope you will marry someone from China, Hong Kong, or even someone from Taiwan. But don't marry a foreigner." I didn't have a boyfriend at the time. The thought of getting married was far from my mind. Stunned, I didn't know how to react to her request for a while. My mind went blank and I said to Mom without thinking, "I am not going to get married then." Relieved and satisfied, Mom tilted her head back against the sofa chair with a huge grin. Dad stood up and came to give me a gentle pat on my head. It was one of the most awkward moments in my life and one I still can remember vividly today. Such a discussion of the topic has never arisen again. My parents had made their points. I got the picture. But could they really control my life? It was up to me now.

Dating or marrying a foreigner in China was unusual in the 1970s and early 1980s. Inter-racial relationships or marriages were seldom talked about in the closed society of that era, and were not accepted by the general public. Occasionally, if such a relationship was discussed, the story would typically be a tragic one. The rumor was that if someone were involved romantically with a foreigner, the Chinese person would not only be looked down upon by his or her family members, but might also end up in jail. It was a socially forbidden relationship at that time. Though the attitude towards inter-racial romance has changed in China in recent decades, prejudice and bias against outsiders has persisted due to centuries of tradition in society.

A few years after that family room drama, I was dating a "white ghost", Terry, in the States. In China during this period of time, the country was going through its early days of economic reform. A new economic policy was in place in the late 1970s after Deng Xiaoping came into power. As the commander of the country, Deng opened up China to foreign trade and investment. As a result, the reform also introduced the people of China to the world and had the effect of opening up Chinese society. People's attitude towards foreigners had also loosened up by the early 1980s. During our first visit to Beijing together, I introduced Terry to my parents as a friend, just a normal friend like many others I had. I stayed with my parents, while Terry found shelter with the help of a friend. The friend was a foreigner like him who was teaching English in Beijing at the time. We went out together with my parents a few times. No questions were asked, and no eyebrows were raised. The last day before leaving for America it was me who wanted to have a nice talk with my parents. Alone without Terry after lunch, I patiently waited until nap time came when we were all lying on a bed in my parents' bedroom. I could hear my heart pounding hard and rapidly. I had no choice; I had to face the fear; my head was spinning. I could choose not to talk to them, yet, I was always honest with them. Besides, I was such a bad liar and any dissembling would be easily detected by them right away. I cleared my throat and said nervously, "You know that guy? I said he was my friend. Actually, he is my boy friend." The room went dead quiet for a moment. You could hear a pin drop.

"We don't know him. But we know you. We trust your judgment," Mom said discreetly after a long pause.

"He is a student who is studying for a master's degree in community and regional planning right now," I went on.

"Em…community planning, eh?" Dad muttered in mild disapproval, as this field did not seem as easily recognizable as medicine, business, or law that would lead to a lucrative career.

That was the end of our conversation. I wondered if Dad really understood what community planning was. Or perhaps he was wondering whether having a planning degree could promise a bright future for his potential son-in-law. Terry didn't choose to be the medical doctor or the lawyer that most of our family friends wished their children to be. Was he good enough for Dad? Nevertheless, I felt extremely grateful to them that day. After all, they trusted my judgment. We got their approval!

I am not sure if by adding a second graduate degree in environmental planning to his resume, Terry has earned himself more or less credit points in the eyes of Dad. Dad isn't against protection of the environment. The subject is simply foreign to him. He isn't willing to invest any effort to explore or understand the importance of it. For a long time, city and environmental planning was anything but a mainstream topic in China. There were never any environmental headlines or big stories on the front pages of the major government newspapers, as far as I can remember. Now I believe that environmental issues have become far more prominent in the minds of Chinese people and in the Chinese media. The fact that Terry loves Chinese food and speaks Chinese helps to gain acceptance points in my family, probably more than his career. His Chinese is at least good enough to allow Dad to relate to him. But Terry, after all, is still a foreigner, a "white ghost". They both speak to each other politely and respectfully, trying to avoid any confrontations if they can. One time during Dad's first visit with Mom in 1991, the back door lock to our house wasn't working well. Dad was eager to fix it for us. Terry went to great ends to explain the problem and showed Dad how to temporarily make it work, just as he would have done for anyone trying to use the door. You had to press the knob down in a specific direction at the same time as turning the lock on or off – a very inconvenient idiosyncrasy! Suddenly the color on Dad's face changed from yellow to red. "I am not a country bumpkin," he said angrily. This was a classic moment in cultural misunderstanding in which Dad had misinterpreted Terry's efforts of explanation about the weird behavior of our lock as patronizing and insulting. Shocked by Dad's unexpected reaction, Terry quickly escaped the awkward situation without saying anything more. Another time Dad was cooking noodles in the kitchen. The noodle soup in the pot over heated; steam and bubbles pushed the lid of the pot up and sizzled onto the stove. While Dad stepped away from the stove for a second, Terry seized the moment, quietly turned the heat down, and walked away. When Dad returned to guard his noodle soup, he quickly noticed it and wasn't pleased. He threw a questionable look behind Terry's back and muttered, "How do you cook food without heat?" Terry quickly learned his lessons and has never interfered with Dad since, letting pots boil over, if necessary, in order to prevent tempers from flaring.

In dealing with any issue involved with Dad and Terry, my method of survival is to be objective and not to interfere. I love them both dearly and don't wish to hurt either of them. Over the years I have been watching the two men make considerable efforts to get to know each other. After cautiously testing the waters first, they have gradually learned to get along. Although occasionally questioning Terry's behavior,

Dad has never openly criticized him in front of me, though once he shook his head when Terry ate an apple without washing it first. Back home in China, you not only have to wash your apples, but also always peel the skins before eating. "Lots of chemicals and pests on the skin," Dad said. He was amazed to see that Terry drinking several cups of milk a day. "People in America drink milk like water," he muttered. It was a special treat if Dad could get hold of milk back then. Milk was rare and expensive during the dry years of the Cultural Revolution and the Chinese Great Leap Forward Movement that resulted in total economic and agricultural collapse. During the period of 1959-1961, China was struck by natural disasters and exacerbated by political interference, resulting in famine throughout the entire country. Millions of people died of starvation. "We grew up eating cabbage. The people here eat too much butter, cheese, and drink too much milk. They have more body fat and body heat than we do," Dad concluded when he spotted Terry, who was only wearing a T-shirt and shorts outdoors in the "cold". One day in the early spring of 2006, during our strolling in the neighborhood, Dad said to me,

"He ought to wear a jacket. It is cold. He will get sick."

"He's okay, Dad. He's strong and used to it."

Staring at the ground that we were about to step on, Dad stopped and remained silent for a few seconds. Then he raised his head, looked directly into my eyes, and said in a serious tone, "You are even whiter than the white people." It was a shock to my face. Where did Dad's emotion come from? Had I just said something that offended him, I puzzled? Speechless, I decided not to respond to Dad's comment. We started pacing ahead slowly on the road again. Occasionally we bumped each other's arms as we moved forward together.

I felt his weight on the concrete road and could hear him breathe heavily. We were so close, yet seemed to be miles away from each other. Our walk ended without any more conversation between us. What more could be said?

That night I was sleepless while searching hard and deep for the meaning behind Dad's comment. I was fully aware that Chinese people still retained a good many misconceptions about westerners, even though the outside world was more accessible to Chinese society in recent decades. I wondered if I had unconsciously transformed myself into a "foreigner". Had certain behaviors of mine triggered Dad's statement? Or perhaps there was something deeper that I was unaware of? How could it be? From the time I landed in America, it had taken me about two years to get used to the flavor and bitterness of coffee. My family routinely drank tea after each meal back home in Beijing. At first I couldn't comprehend why people in the States loved coffee so much. To me it was black with an awfully bitter taste, like Chinese herbal medicine. A memory of taking Chinese medicine flashed in my mind. As a child, if I got sick my parents always treated my symptoms with Chinese herbals that tasted bitter and were hard to swallow. I resisted the black juice first, but eventually had to give in holding my nose and quickly flushed the bitter liquid down my throat. "The more bitter, the better it is," Dad told me. I was led to believe that Chinese herbs were wonder drugs that would magically heal me. I have learned that bitter isn't necessarily a bad thing. Like Chinese herbal medicine, coffee is a wonder drug for the Americans. I can't remember how I began my habit of drinking coffee. I might have tried a cup or two one day as an experiment, then decided I could take it, and later began loving it. There are so many gourmet coffee shops in this country. It was easier to get a cup of coffee than to get a cup of jasmine or green tea years ago when tea wasn't as popular as today. I've become so used to coffee that I prefer coffee over tea now. Does drinking coffee make me white?

When I first arrived here, I couldn't comprehend why people in the States consider sandwiches as serious food. The space between two pieces of bread was stuffed with anything from vegetable leaves to pieces of meat. "What a kind of crazy food is this?" Dad said, shaking his head with disapproval. I am now one of those people who enjoy eating sandwiches. Even worse, according to Dad I can go camping and eat sandwiches without thinking about Chinese food for days. Sometimes I pack a sandwich for lunch when I go to work. A Chinese friend once told me, "I have never seen any Chinese people who like sandwiches as much as you do." I simply responded to her, "I am used to it." Does enjoying eating a sandwich make me whiter?

Once I attended a Chinese New Year party at a friend's house. People at the party were mostly my childhood friends now living in the States. There was a medical research lab technician, a self-employed acupuncturist, a biotech researcher, a computer scientist, a mechanical engineer turned into a self-made construction builder, a former office clerk at the Chinese Academy of Sciences, as well as their in-laws and parents. Besides the compliments regarding the comfortable home and the delicious Chinese food the host provided, the conversations at the party were devoted entirely to the topics of Chinese DVD movies and various drama series that they had been watching religiously every night. They also talked about the recent books they had exchanged among themselves, as well as the major news events that they had observed on the Mandarin news channel. I admitted to them that I was unaware of the DVD movies, ignorant about the

Chinese drama, and preferred to watch my news on PBS and CNN channels instead. I created an instant scene of shock and disbelief at the party. Everybody's head turned in my direction. The host of the party gazed at me harshly and questioned me firmly, "Wei, are you Chinese?" Her remark sent an electrical shock wave down my spine. Everyone was affected by the lightning filling the air. I thought, boy, I didn't intend to upset the host. Though I grew up with some of the people at the party, they didn't really know me, did they? We had grown apart in America. If Dad were here at the party, he would have been ashamed of me. To some of my Chinese friends, I am already white and no longer one of them.

Ironically, I am never white enough for my western colleagues. After twenty years of working in the same office, some of my colleagues still haven't figured out a way to relate to me. My exchanges with them involve both verbal and non-verbal communication. It seems to me that my face reminds them of China and leads to discussions on international affairs or internal Chinese policies. Though I am flattered, the truth is that I don't really follow the Chinese news. I have already lived half of my life in America. China is out of reach and quite foreign to me now. I often wonder if those colleagues still perceive me as a stranger. After years of working together, don't they have other things to say to me instead of talking about China? I remember once a colleague was going to attend a James Taylor concert during the weekend. As we discussed our weekend activities, she tested me.

"I don't know if you have heard of James Taylor."

"What about him?"

"I am going to his concert this weekend."

"Wow! I really like his slow guitar ballads, especially the one about the lonely cowboy singing to the cow herd in the moon light. And of course, there is the pensive and regretful "Fire and Rain.""

She seemed to be surprised and uncomfortable that I was familiar with this western musical icon. I had responded to her politely, but felt awkward inside. Was I overreacting to her questions? I wasn't ignorant even though I wasn't born in this country, I thought. I am sure that a lot of native born Americans are not aware of James Taylor's music. Was I too sensitive and too insecure, I wondered? I am sure my colleague meant well. I have a tendency to think too much when being questioned about American culture.

One day I was in a restaurant with a few friends. An elderly gentleman sitting at the table next to ours stood up and walked forwards me. "Are you Chinese?" he asked in a friendly tone. "Yup. I'm from Beijing." Delighted, he told me about his memorable visit to China recently. I have experienced similar situations many times before. No matter how good my English is, or how much I know about American pop culture, or how often I enjoy drinking coffee or eating sandwiches, or how white, according to my Chinese friends, I can be, I always get the same question, "Where are you from?" If I happen to feel doom and gloom, my answer to it can be playful. It generally goes like this:

"Where are you from?"

"I'm from Ann Arbor, Michigan."

"Em…em...eh?"

"Before that, I was in Lincoln, Nebraska."

"Em…."

"But, I originally came from Beijing, China."

The questioner finally gets to the bottom and leaves with satisfaction. It is a friendly question, I suppose. I find myself overreacting to the situation again and again. Why do those people assume I am a foreigner? Is it because I look Asian? What about the people who are of Asian decent and who were born here? Do they have to answer the same question as I do? After all, this country is supposed to be a "melting pot" consisting of citizens of all races, from all parts of the world. This is what makes America great as a country, isn't it?

In the eyes of Dad and my Chinese friends, I am as white as snow. To my Caucasian friends and some of my colleagues, I am not *Snow White*. I wonder if there is an "identity operation" involved in being an immigrant to this country. That is, perhaps one has to constantly go through a lifelong process of modification and self-transformation. Perhaps in doing so, one has to combine one's adapted culture with one's own identity in order to derive a third element as a means of adapting to change and defining one's distinct cultural identity. "To do in Rome as Romans do" is the saying that I have taken to heart as my guiding light to brighten my passage in times of difficulty. To succeed in an unknown territory, my gut tells me the importance of building survival skills, understanding a different culture rather than my own, blending myself into the current society that I now belong to, and learning more about the culture that is enriched by heritages of ethnic groups and Native Americans who had lived on this land for centuries before the Caucasians came. To learn the unknowns, to truly know who you are and where you come from, is my slogan. The principle of always keeping my dignity and retaining my own identity is my compass that guides me through my life long journey. One must draw strength from one's own cultural roots and from one's adopted society. This land is your land and mine as well. I am an American. This is my home. I am neither white nor yellow. I am who I am.

11. Being a Fellow

Wei at the 2007 SLA conference

One cold January afternoon in 2007, my office phone rang. I picked it up and heard a soft, unfamiliar voice on the other side.

"Is it Wei?"

"Yes."

"This is Rebecca, the President of the Special Libraries Association."

"Hi Rebecca, what can I do for you?"

"Congratulations, Wei. You have just been named as a Fellow of the association."

"What?"

"Yes. You have become a new fellow of the association. The honor will be presented to you before Al Gore's keynote speech at the 2007 annual conference. The detailed information regarding the ceremony will be sent to you from the headquarters later. There will be a press release," Rebecca went on with enthusiasm.

"Umm...Thank you," feeling numb for a moment, I finally responded to her, but couldn't hear my own voice.

After years of serving the professional society of Special Librarians, I thought I deserved it, but I had never actually expected it. The news was surreal. This was a great honor given to me by my peers. I couldn't conceive how high I had just reached in my personal journey to a successful career. The 2007 conference theme was Climbing to New Heights, which sounded timely. Life has its highs and lows and is a theater of changes and turns depending on each stage of a scene. One can hardly imagine where a drama might begin or end.

I was in my early teens when the Cultural Revolution began in 1966. The revolution that ended in 1976, after Mao's death, was an attempt by Mao to re-establish his power over the party and the country. Mao mobilized the Red Guards, which consisted of thousands of students and youths, to spearhead an attack on the "bourgeoisie". They took over schools, factories, companies, and government organizations, and moved into people's private homes. The entire country seemed to be in the hands of the Red Guards. Led by the Red Guards, people from all corners of the country traveled by train or on foot to the east, west, north, and south to spread Chairman Mao's words. The country became a gigantic network. Wherever you wanted to go, you could do so individually or with a group of Red Guards, especially during the early stages of the revolution. Everyone wanted to join the Guards and to be a part of the action.

The Red Guard commander at my middle school was two years older than me. One afternoon, a few months into the revolution, we had a serious talk in the hallway of the school building. Besides me and the commander, no one else was there at the time. Along the walls on each side of the long and narrow hallway, there were huge posters about corruption of the school officials and teachers, along with huge slogans supporting Mao and the revolution. The commander made it clear to me that he was in charge, and informed me that I wasn't qualified to be a Red Guard. The reason? My parents were capitalists, according to him. No sons and daughters of capitalists were allowed to be a part of this prestigious group. Ashamed of myself and my family background, I was sad that I had been overlooked and rejected.

Yet I was determined to participate in the movement, to be a part of the real action. Transportation was freely provided; everyone around me seemed to be on the go. The whole country was moving. The Red Guards called it "big networking," (*Da chuan lian*). I didn't want to be left behind, even though I was not a Red Guard. My parents were under pressure to confess their wrong doings by the Guards. They lost their positions and were ordered to do manual labor every day. Therefore they had no time to look after my brother and me. I decided to join the action and to take a free ride. It was hip; it would make me look good and feel good if I traveled.

Ling Ling, my friend, also belonged to my category. She was one year older than me and became my traveling companion and "partner in crime". The Red Guards traveled by train implementing their clear mission. Ling Ling and I had no idea where we were heading, had no fear, but just wanted to go somewhere. We said good-bye to our parents and left for the Beijing train station. The station was chaotic and crowded when we arrived. A passenger train heading south was parked on the tracks, motionless. Each car was jammed with people sitting like sardines in a can. We found a car towards the end of the train in the hope that it had room for a few more passengers. By the time we reached the car entrance, it was already blocked by hot, frenzied bodies. There was no way we could get in except by climbing up the car and entering through the windows. Someone inside lent us a helping hand. We grabbed the hand and managed to get through a narrow window one at the time. Once inside, we discovered that there were no empty seats for us to sit on. Even the corridor was also occupied by bodies and luggage on top of each other. We stepped on people, pushed our way through the crowd, and finally found a small space in a corner near the bathroom. We had a tiny spot to rest our legs, just in time for the announcement made by the conductor. "The final destination of the train is Shaoshan, Hunan province, Chairman Mao's home town." The train suddenly struck up a lively tune. Great! Now we knew where we would be heading to. Shaoshan, Mao's birthplace, was the destination where everybody would disembark; there were no other stops along the way. "Shaoshan will provide us with a great education," the conductor went on proudly. Even the food on the train was free, as it was at Shaoshan. Where did they get the money to pay for the expenses, I pondered? The country must have paid a great price for this great education. Meanwhile, I was happy to ride the rails. When we arrived at Shaoshan early the next morning, several trucks were already waiting for us at the train station. We were all bused right away to Mao's birthplace, now a museum in the village of Shaoshan. In front of his childhood home, I got hold of a bowl of streamed rice with a few slices of pickled daikon on top, freely distributed to us all. I don't really know who provided us with the free breakfast. Perhaps it was from the museum run by the local government. The meal was not a typical breakfast I would have had in Beijing. Nevertheless, I quickly wolfed down my tasteless and dry breakfast to fill my empty stomach. Soon after the breakfast, we were led on an extensive tour starting at the entrance of the museum. We also saw Mao's family compound, where we were each given a Red Book before the tour that contained Mao's wisdom and quotations. On this trip we had learned once again that Mao was our great leader and the God of the country. We all worshiped him wholeheartedly. After one night of free lodging, Ling Ling and I climbed up onto the free train and headed back north to our home in Beijing.

One winter morning after my educational trip to Shaoshan, I heard piercing screams from the third floor above. The sudden disturbance broke the peace and quiet of a cold morning and sent chills of apprehension down my spine. The loud cries were from Grandma Liu upstairs. Liu had been living with her son and his family on the third floor for years. She was polite and quiet and always seemed to keep to herself. In the past, if I ran into her in the apartment building shared by several households, I would say hi, but had never really got to know her. From her yelling, I managed to understand that her son had just jumped to his death from the third floor, landing on the concrete ground in front of the building. I could hear her footsteps going up and down the stairs accompanied by crying, screaming, howling, and pleading for help. Most adults were at work; no one came out to help. My brother and I were home alone, but we were scared to go out. I had never seen a dead body before and didn't want to see one now. We locked ourselves inside for the whole day. We were later told by the adults that the body of Grandma Liu's son was removed from the front entrance of the apartment building by officials earlier that day.

For the next a couple of days after Liu's suicide, my brother and I were still afraid to use the front entrance of the building. We ended up getting in and out through the windows. Although the body had been removed, Grandma Liu's cries didn't stop. Her chilling cries continued throughout the day, permeating the entire complex. Echoes of her sorrow traveled through the entire building for more than two weeks. I later heard that her daughter-in-law refused to let her into the house. Grandma pounded the door and pleaded for shelter and food every day. Suddenly one day, the pounding stopped in the hallway upstairs. The building became quiet again, but the incident haunted me for a long time afterwards. I never found out from my parents why Grandma Liu's son had jumped to his death or what a kind of "crime" he had committed. I only learned much later that many innocent people like her son died without committing any wrong doing during the revolution. These people were punished simply because they had questioned Mao's policy and the party's authority. Dad told me later that Grandma Liu's daughter-in-law didn't want her to live with the family any more. She wanted to cut off all ties and connections with Grandma. She was afraid that she, too, would be accused of being a capitalist. Grandma Liu had no one and no place to go since she had depended solely on his son's financial support. Dad never found out where she went afterwards. Years later, when I asked Dad about Grandma Liu again, Dad simply said to me, "I heard she died soon after that tragic incident." I wondered what Mao would say or do if he had learned about the incident. As the God of the country, would he have found a place for Grandma Liu to stay? Could he have helped Grandma to find her strength and inner peace again? Could he have saved Grandma Liu and rescue her only son from this madness?

Family photo taken before leaving for Inner Mongolia

Two years after Grandma Liu's disappearance, I was told by the authorities to pack my bag and get myself re-educated by peasants in Inner Mongolia. A few weeks after Dad and

I had broken down and cried our eyes out in my bedroom on a summer afternoon, I was on a train that would be slowly moving away from the capital train station in the direction of the grasslands extending to the northern border of China, where the richest and largest concentration of natural resources in the country, such as coal, alkali, asbestos and mica are found. As more people boarded the train, I heard quiet sobbing as well as loud, convulsive gasps throughout the entire car. With my teary eyes, I hunted for the noises around me. I recognized most of the faces belonging to people between the ages of twelve and sixteen from the same school I had attended. All of a sudden the steam locomotive uttered a loud steamy sigh as dark smoke whistled up the engine's chimney. The train slowly chugged into motion, issuing more puffs of steam and rapidity accelerated to the north. The Beijing train station became smaller and smaller, gradually disappearing into the horizon behind me as the shedding of tears subsided. We all started eating and sharing the food packed for us by our parents. I opened a plastic container Mom had stuck into my carry-on backpack an hour before we left for the train station from home that morning. In it I discovered fried Chinese noodles and a boiled egg that I normally got for my birthday. Today was not an occasion for celebration of my birthday. Was it their way of showing how much they loved and cared about me? Noodles and eggs were supposed to bring good luck to me, as I was told on my birthday by my parents each year. With the best wishes from my parents, I was prepared to try my luck in Inner Mongolia.

Every object around me seemed to be brown, yellow, and dusty, including the bright morning sky. I stepped out of the train and landed my feet on the home ground of Genghis Khan (1162-1227), the brilliant and fearless leader of Mongolians. Where was natural beauty and vast grasslands

WEI WEI

so often portrayed in printed landscapes that had fascinated me? Where were the yurts and the herds of sheep moving like white clouds on the remote, rolling grasslands often portrayed in folk songs? I quickly hopped onto the open truck that awaited us. It started ahead to the village where I was going to live and work. The truck and its passengers were ready to take on the challenges presented by road bumps, dust, and dirt. About twenty minutes into our journey, we encountered our first village. As the truck passed through the village slowly, I spotted a group of young kids playing with stones on the dirt in front of their doorsteps. No adults were present. The truck seemed to catch the kids by surprise as it moved closer. The peaceful village was suddenly inundated by joyful shouts. Calling for attention, the kids stopped the game and started waving to us. The truck sent up clouds of dust from behind. The kids began running after it until their red, dirty faces with runny noses, their little body covered with shabby clothes, all disappeared in the cloudy air. I couldn't remember how long we had been rolling back and forth on the truck that kept moving. We must have spent a long time traveling to the village. Here winter was cold and very long with frequent blizzards, and summer was short and warm. Here I would be weeding a vegetable plot, pawing my way through the endless wheat fields, harvesting corn for both human and livestock, and spending the next three years of my life re-educating myself.

I was taught in school early in my life that religion, like opium, could drug one's mind and soul. Religion was only for those who had a weak spot in their soul. Only Mao and Marxism could save mankind. Karen greeted me at my doorstep two days after I had landed in Omaha, Nebraska, more than a decade after Inner Mongolia. She looked pale, had blond hair, and was pretty in a white summer dress. She looked like a gothic figure in picture books or portrayed in movies. Karen passed a Bible to me and followed with an invitation to attend her church on Sundays. I explained to Karen that it was impossible for me to believe in anyone or anything. After all, I had just experienced the Cultural Revolution and had studied Mao's Red Book. I wasn't in a worship mood. Karen was patient and soft spoken and insisted on having me attend her church on Sundays. She must have been disappointed in me, since I went with her only once. Karen was persistent, but I held my ground and resisted her efforts. By the time I moved from Omaha to Lincoln, we became friends.

Karen paid me a few visits in Lincoln where I had rented a one-bedroom unit in a two story apartment building close to downtown and the university campus. On the first floor of the building there was a music shop where all manner of instruments, vinyl records, and cassette tapes were sold. The second floor was divided into individual units all occupied by foreign students, mostly from China, Thailand, and other developing countries. The rent for these units was affordable. My unit was old and also occupied by armies of cockroaches. One midsummer Friday, Karen came for a visit from Omaha. After dinner we were invited to join a group of friends at a local bar. Karen insisted on staying behind. Having no success in changing her mind, I joined my friends without her. It was hot that night. When I came back around midnight, Karen was still up and reading in the living room. There was no air conditioning in my unit. All the windows were wide open, inviting outdoor breezes to cool down the room temperature. I was sorry that Karen had missed the fun, but she said she felt perfectly content herself with a book. We then went to bed right away.

Karen and I shared the bed in my room that night. I was tired but restless and couldn't fall asleep for a long time. Just as I was dozing in and out of sleep, I heard a sound close to the bedroom door. Half awake, I saw that the bedroom door was moving, gradually and slowly opening. Could it be Karen? My sleepy brain pondered the situation; my eyes were struggling to focus on the door that was moving. Through the moonlight from the window I spotted a man, a stranger, crawling on his hands and knees, dragging his body close to the floor and slowly moving towards us. He was a medium sized white male. As he was crawling closer and closer to the bed, I could see that he had a pale face and brown hair. Lying on bed, I was stunned, and wanted to say something to Karen, but I could neither open my mouth, nor move my body muscles. I was so paralyzed by the stranger that for a moment I didn't feel Karen by my side. What was Karen doing? Did she see the intruder? I wondered as the thoughts jumped through my mind. Now the man was only inches away from the bed. Still low on the ground, he lifted his hands from the floor quietly, then quickly opened them up. Like a cat, he was ready to pounce. Just as he was about to jump, Karen suddenly sat up and screamed. She must have yelled something to the man, but I was too shocked to catch anything that she had said. Karen screamed her lungs out. Later she told me her voice hurt for few days.

The intruder stared at us for a second, then sharply turned around and ran out the door. We quickly got out of bed, noticing that all the windows to the living room and the main door were wide open. The phone lines and electrical wires had been cut, disabling the lights and the phone. We rushed to a neighbor and called the police. During this whole ordeal I was so impressed by Karen's bravery. Both of us were scared at that moment, but it was Karen who had conquered her fear and acted promptly. I often wonder where Karen got her strength from that night. Was it from her God? If Karen had not been there on that fateful night, what would have happened to me? Was God watching over us down from above? Had we been protected by God's spirit on that unforgettable night? Karen and I only saw each other briefly again afterwards. As the years have gone by, we have lost contact. I have no idea where Karen's God is leading her in life. In my memory, Karen was a true Christian and a brave warrior to her God.

Bill, a medium-built, generous man, was a chemist in his fifties. He had grey hair, a grey mustache, and often rode a motorcycle to work. I got acquainted with him through his daughter at the university in Lincoln, Nebraska, where we both studied. Bill was also an art collector, and was especially fond of Native American art and artifacts. He displayed his collections mostly on the walls of his suburban home. He was a friendly fellow, and from time to time would host parties for the local Chinese students at his house. I had attended several of Bill's parties, which provided a networking opportunity that allowed the seasoned students to embrace the newcomers. It was also a place for us to check in with each other regarding our daily lives. Shan, who recently arrived from China, was a bright and intelligent young man who had just enrolled to get his PhD in American literature. I met Shan at one of Bill's parties and later ran into him a few times in between the classes at school. Our conversations were usually brief. One Saturday night I was invited to Bill's potluck party. Shan was there with his new wife, Fairy, who had come from China a month before. Fairy was slender, with long shining black hair. She had an egg-shaped face and big round eyes with long eyelashes. She seemed to be in her late twenties. According to Chinese standards, Fairy was a true beauty. Since Shan and I were in the same department, I wanted to get to know both of them better. We discussed the elective classes offered by the department and Shan talked to me about his area of focus and his potential dissertation topic. Fairy stood there patiently listening to our conversation. She later said that once she had settled down, she too would like to pursue a degree at the university. What a bright couple, I thought. Everyone at the party that night was in good spirits. After supper we sang Chinese folk songs while Bill and his daughter took turns playing piano. It ended on a high note. I said bye to Shan and Fairy, promising to talk to them again soon.

In the late afternoon of the next day, while I was reading in the living room, the phone rang. A friend broke the sad news that Fairy, Shan's new wife, had died in a bicycle accident that morning. According to the news circulated among the local Chinese students, early in the morning Fairy was riding a bike on her way to work on the north campus. It was around the crack of dawn and visibility was poor. The pavement of the streets was still very wet from the heavy rain the previous night. Fairy was riding on the road side when a truck approached her. The driver of the truck, while fumbling for her coffee cup, lost focus on the road. After a few seconds the coffee cup was in her hand. As she was ready to take a sip, she suddenly spotted Fairy, but it was too late. She hit Fairy, who was taken to the local hospital and died shortly thereafter.

The news hit me hard, even though I barely knew her. I had just met her at Bill's party the night before. Now she was gone forever. In mere few seconds, the truck driver tragically took Fairy's young life. Fairy's image was so vigorous in my memory; I couldn't help thinking of her and that last party we enjoyed together at Bill's. How could a lively soul be gone, out of existence on the Earth in a blink of eye? I could still feel her presence and hear her soft voice. In an imaginary moment, I reached out my hands to touch her, but she was not there. She seemed to be so close to me, yet so far away, up in the air, in heaven. Fairy would have had a great future. She would have lived with Shan happily together in America. Her hopes and dreams in this new found land had instantly vanished. Being the only child in her family, how did her parents receive the devastating news in China? Shan must have also been heart broken by the sudden death of his new wife. These thoughts came to my mind as I was sitting in the living room alone that afternoon, as clouds floated across the brilliant blue sky. I wondered if Fairy was still here with us. She reminded me of a goddess in a Chinese fairy tale. Fairy's soul had floated to the sky, to the moon where a beautiful Chinese girl called Chang'e has been living for over 4,000 years. Chang'e is the Chinese moon goddess and Fairy had joined her up there on the moon. I was sleepless that night and lost my appetite for a month. I sent my condolences to Shan later and didn't hear from him or ever run into him again before I left Nebraska.

I have fond memories of Nebraska, where I met some memorable characters. Another one of them was Jerome. Jerome was a muscular and confident man in his forties, a typical out-going, loud, and showy American. He had playful eyes and always wore a shallow-brimmed hat. Besides divorcing East Indian and Japanese wives, he had also dated a Native American woman, and finally settled down with his good wife, Ann, who is white. Jerome has a rare quality, a constitution mixed equally with muscles and brain. He is a body builder, a tree trimmer, a literature PhD, and a professor of literature who writes beautiful poems. I met Jerome at a party. He stopped by later and said "hi" at my work at the university cafeteria where I was serving Sloppy Joes. When Terry joined me in Nebraska, the three of us became instant friends. As poor as church mice, we would pinch pennies to save for a feast. The biggest events for us during the weekends were our jaunts to Denny's, eight blocks away from the campus. We also indulged occasionally in delicious local pizza if we had extra money in our pockets. Together we not only tripped the light fantastic, but also debated global current affairs, movie plots, and movie characters. We also critiqued books that we had recently read. Our lively and heated discussions aroused in ourselves much curiosity. I was longing to learn more about American culture, its heritage, and the Midwest with its rich oral histories of Plains Indians, great explorers, and pioneers.

Nebraska, the Cornhusker State, is more beautiful than one can envision. It is a place of subtle natural wonder and beauty, with rolling sand hills, intriguing prairie potholes, the historic Platte River, the wild and scenic Niobrara, wooded bluffs, and verdant grasslands. It is hot in summer, cold and snowy in winter, and famous for its lightning-blinding, ear-shattering thunderstorms and devastating tornadoes that often occur during the spring and summer. Nebraska is the place where I discovered Willa Cather's *O Pioneers!* and *My Ántonia*. It is the place where I learned about John Neihardt, whose *Black Elk Speaks*, a story of an Oglala Sioux medicine man, has touched me deeply. It is also the place where Frances, Paul, and Charlie, professors on my graduate council, introduced me to the literary works by Margaret Laurence as well as Ole Edvart Rolvaag's *Giants in the Earth*, a story of a Norwegian immigrant family that I later completed my thesis on.

A memory of this time period stands strong in my mind to this day. I was requested to discuss in my thesis the theory of

Soren Kierkegaard, a nineteenth-century Danish philosopher and theologian, with Paul, a notable Kierkegaard scholar. One day I found him in his office, furnished with a simple desk, a wooden desk chair, a sofa, and shelves upon shelves of books. Paul was plain-looking, of medium build, with sensitive eyes, and seemed older and wiser than his actual age. Wearing a loose white cotton shirt and a pair of blue khaki pants, he was busy writing at his desk. I stuck my head into his open doorway and asked respectfully,

"Sorry to trouble you, Paul. Do you have a minute?"

"Sure, come in," he said, then stopped writing and left his pen on top of a sheet of white paper.

"I am told you are a well-known scholar of Kierkegaard. I'd like to learn from you."

"I still don't know much about him. Let's learn together."

Paul turned his head, responding to my request with a sincere smile. He was humble about his stature as one of field's most influential and respected scholars. I was deeply moved, as I much later stepped out of Paul's office with a list of scholarly books on the topic. What a great lesson it would be for me to learn from him, I thought. I could never forget his simple, humble response. Learning is a lifelong process. Once you think you know all, you immediately stop learning. There is an old Chinese saying, "If you know ten, you say you only know five," (*Zhi dau shi, zhi shuo wu*). One is respected and admired if one is humble. Paul has truly gained my admiration. A year later when the *Lincoln Star*, a local newspaper, published a front page article highlighting my study and my life at the university, I felt humbled. I thought of Paul and wondered what he would think if he were in my shoes. Perhaps he would simply say, "Thank you. I am just doing my job to try to make the world a better place." Paul probably didn't realize the great impact of what he had said to me in his office that day. It became a guiding light that accompanied me through my studies and throughout my professional career later on. He not only taught me how to be a good scholar, but also how to be true to myself.

Following graduation from the English Masters Program at the University of Nebraska, Lincoln, I decided to pursue more practical endeavors and ended up choosing the field of Information Science. After submitting applications to various colleges, I selected the University of Michigan, Ann Arbor, for its fine reputation and also because of its University of Library Associates Program, a unique work-study combination. My Ann Arbor years flew by faster than one can imagine. Patricia, head of the Natural Science Library at the time, had more faith in me than I had it in myself. It was she who encouraged me to earn a graduate degree in information science, which I was later able to use in an academic setting.

Before coming to Ann Arbor, Patricia interviewed me for a position at the university library associate's program, a prestigious graduate program which had only selected nine students nationwide that year. When I questioned my own ability to work as a library associate in a science field at the university, it was she who said to me, "If I can do it you can do it also, as long as you are willing to learn the science vocabulary and work hard." I have never looked back after that conversation and have marched on. Whenever I had doubts about my ability to fulfill an academic career, or was caught in the middle of a political conflict in a working environment, her remarks were always in the back of my mind, and have often served to motivate me in times of doubt or difficulty. Conversely, in times of success and triumph, Patricia's guiding words have reminded me to be grounded. In failure, they reminded me to stand up and keep going. Mentors like Paul and Patricia serve as my professional back bone. They have supported and inspired me at different stages of my life when I needed to grow and be pushed further. They taught me to understand that learning is a never-ending process. I am fortunate to have met many beneficent and intelligent people like Paul and Patricia in my life and in my professional career.

During my graduate work at Ann Arbor, I was introduced to my professional society, the Special Libraries Association (SLA), and have been involved in it ever since. It provides me with management opportunities and a training ground where I have sharpened my professional skills, and later put what I have learned into practice in my daily routines. The association consists of information professionals worldwide, and provides a huge network among peers. We come together and exchange new ideas at different locations annually. We learn from each other about new technical tools that can enhance the field of the information profession. The respect shown to me by my professional community also makes me feel comfortable about who I am. Thus, my nomination and bestowal of the prestigious title of SLA Fellow by my peers was a great honor and beyond my wildest dreams. I could never have envisioned receiving such an honor when I was on the train to Mao's birthplace in Shaoshan during the Cultural Revolution, when I was doing manual labor in the corn fields of Inner Mongolia, or when I was on the plane to San Francisco in 1981. I am living a dream that my parents could have never imagined.

When I brought home the good news of my becoming a new fellow of SLA after work that day, Dad was naturally excited about the news. The sinking sunlight penetrated the encircling redwoods, slowing shrouding the mysteries of the surrounding nature on that cold but beautiful late afternoon, as we paced slowly through the neighborhood after supper. I asked Dad, "Would you like to be in Denver in June when my society presents the award to me at the conference?" "Yes," Dad answered me with a broad grin. His creased face was softened by the glow of dimming sunlight. He remained quiet without saying much more after that, but his smile said it all on that walk.

Dad seldom praised me, at least not that I can remember. In Denver, during the awards ceremony minutes before the former Vice President Al Gore's keynote speech, Dad was sitting there in the front row of the conference ballroom. He was watching me on center stage, accepting my honor from my peers, who numbered in the thousands in a standing-room-only auditorium. I knew at that very moment that Dad was indeed proud of me. At the time, it didn't matter if he could understand the video showing the highlights of my professional career, nor if he could comprehend a single word the SLA president said about my professional accomplishments. Sometimes understanding is able to transgress language boundaries. I knew that in his heart he had translated into his own language every word said on that stage. He understood how hard that I had worked and how far that I had traveled on my personal journey. At that very moment, we both knew that Mom was watching. She was looking down and smiling from the heavens. She was saying to me, "You did a good job! Well done!" "*Gong xi, gong xi*", a Chinese phrase meaning "congratulations".

12. Marching with Mao

In April of 2008, after his recent visit to Beijing, Dad frequently complained about the rigors of aging. He was only seventy-eight, but insisted his real age was seventy-nine. In Mainland China, people often say they are one year older than they actually are. Traditionally, Chinese people count their age beginning from birth as already being one year old. Every Chinese lunar year that you traverse counts for one more year from your birth age of one.

"You are only seventy-eight, Dad," I disagreed with Dad's method of counting his age, while we paced through the neighborhood one day.

"I spent my first year in my mom's tummy. Once I was born, I was already two years old," Dad explained.

"But you are still young, Dad. It is always important for a person to feel young at heart.".

"I am no longer young. My health is waning. I can feel it," Dad muttered.

"I once saw an elderly man who seemed to be in his seventies who had hiked all the way up to the top of the Yosemite Falls once." I was trying to find a role model for him.

"These foreigners grew up eating cheese and drinking milk, while we were surviving on cabbage and rice. They have stronger bones than we do," Dad made an excuse that I knew I had heard before.

"It's not too late. You could live to be one hundred if you ate well, exercised often, and took care of yourself." I attempted to motivate him.

"Oh, your brother told me I could only live to eighty years old," Dad retorted.

"You need to enjoy every single day of your life. You've got to live. Don't just sit and wait for your death," I pleaded.

"I am getting old. Physically I am degenerating," Dad responded, shaking his head.

Dad's remarks about being old irritate me. Beyond taking pity on him, or no matter whether I agree or disagree with his method of counting the years, his current state of mind regarding his low expectations for the later years of his life saddens me deeply. According to Dad, eighty is a big number in one's life that marks a turning point and symbolizes the beginning of the end. I suppose that one can either enjoy one's remaining life, or sit around and wait for the end. Living in America, I have seen a number of seniors in their seventies or eighties still enjoying outdoor activities and traveling around the world. At my health club, I became acquainted with a strong and determined Swiss American woman in her late seventies who still went downhill skiing every winter and swam in the pool every day. Her advanced years had hardly slowed her down. It grieves me that Dad is constantly reminding everyone that he is already near the end of his life. As for an outlook of aging, I am not sure if there is a cultural difference between Chinese and Americans. Regardless of race, gender, and cultural background, does everyone feel the same as Dad does once reaching eighty years of age? Does one's attitude play a more important role in how one ages, or even how fast the body deteriorates?

Dad's sober mood infiltrated my blood and veins. I felt an urge to learn more about his earlier years as a young man. In the summer of 2008 I taped my interviews with Dad after our daily evening walk. He told me how, in September 1937, China was under full-scale attack from Japan. However, the countryside of Shaanxi Province would remain mostly under control of the Red Army. Throughout the remainder of the Anti-Japanese War, the Red Army engaged in guerrilla and large scale attacks, trying to disrupt Japanese communications and transport on the Yellow River within Shaanxi Province. Between 1937 and the mid-1940s, China fought heavy battles against the Japanese aggressor, experienced a long period of struggle for their very existence, and suffered heavy losses. In the end, however, Chinese determination paid off and the Japanese were defeated. Among the many twists and turns in Dad's life, the experience that struck me the most was the time when he was marching with Mao after 1945, the year in which the Japanese militarists sounded the note of unconditional surrender.

News about the surrender of the Japanese troops had broken at the Red Army base in Shaanxi Province, where Dad was stationed. After years of a bloody Anti-Japanese War, everyone was joyous that the suffering and violence had finally come to an end. Soldiers and citizens in the liberated areas celebrated the defeat of Japan and the victory of Red Army in Yan'an. They were dancing and singing on the streets; the celebration lasted for three days. After the Japanese surrender in 1945, Dad was sent by his army unit for training at the

Telecommunication School in Yan'an for about a half year. The civil war between the Nationalists and Communists had escalated soon after World War II. According to Mao's spokesman for the Communist Party at the time, and in Dad's recollection, the Nationalists ordered a concentrated attack on the Red Army and liberated areas. The areas under siege included "eastern China, the Central Plains, northern China, the Northwest, and the Northeast". All the large cities in these areas were "occupied" by the Nationalist "troops at one time or another." The Red Army troops started retreating from Yan'an, its central headquarters. Yan'an was short of labor. Dad was among three other people selected to work for the central telecommunication station that belonged to the headquarters in the city of Yan'an, from where the Red Army directed all its troops in the war zones.

Dad was with a group of forty people, including Mao, during that time at Yan'an. Most of the people in the group were either Mao's key advisors or his assistants. Zhou En Lai, later the Prime Minister of the People's Republic China after 1949, was also in the group. A part of Dad's unit was in charge of the telecommunications for the entire Red Army, which served a vital function as the Red Army began to withdraw from its war zones to avoid Nationalist troops.

Though Mao's headquarters consisted of forty people stationed in Yan'an, they all had to move around frequently from place to place in the neighboring Shaanxi rural areas not far from Yan'an to escape the Nationalist Army. The search intensified; the Nationalist Army sent its Shaanxi local troops to hunt for Mao day and night. The strategy of Mao's headquarters was to stay away from the cities and hide out in the mountainous areas or small villages. Mao's tactics were very simple, as Dad explained: "The enemy advances, we retreat. The enemy camps, we harass. The enemy tires, we attack. The enemy retreats, we pursue." Dad and other group members walked every day regardless of heavy rains or other inclement weather. The Nationalist Army thought Mao's group had already crossed the Yellow River, which straddles the Shanxi-Shaanxi border, but in fact, Mao was still in the Shaanxi area. As soon as Mao's headquarters had learned that the Nationalist Army was near, they were immediately on the move. "We played chess games with our enemy; most of the time they had no idea where we were," Dad said.

The Red Army also engaged the enemy troops in Shandong Province, and the Hubei region which encompasses several northern and the northeast provinces of China, which had already been liberated. In order to divert their enemies and enable them to send more troops and supplies to the war zones, Mao's forty soldiers were holding many more than their own numbers of the Nationalist Army on the ground in Shaanxi. Dad was with Mao, Zhou, and other well-known leaders every day. They were moving around and on the go all the time from the spring of 1947 to March of 1948. They walked during the day and sometimes marched at night. They had to move on as soon as the Nationalist Army was spotted within a few miles of them. If they had a chance to rest, they would sleep in a fields of crops. The group of forty had only one horse and it was for Mao. The rest of the men, including Zhou, tread on bare feet. The goal of the Nationalist Army was to catch Mao. They learned that Mao was somewhere close, but they didn't know exactly where he was. There were a couple of close encounters with the enemy as Mao's group marched. Sometimes the two hostile opponents were only a few miles away from each other. Mao's group was in a deep valley and could often see the enemy climbing up in the mountains. The places where Mao's headquarters were stationed along the way were kept top secret. After Mao's troops had occupied one place, they left no traces or evidence behind, not even a piece of paper. The enemy could find neither hide nor hair of Mao. "The villagers in the liberated areas were very good about keeping our whereabouts secret," said Dad. "They worshiped Mao and were very kind to us. Lots of times we slept outside their door steps because we did not want to disturb them." By late March of 1948, the group of forty had crossed the Yellow River. After crossing this famous river, they left Shaanxi for the region historically known as Jin, Chahar, and Ji which now mainly comprise Shanxi, Inner Mongolia, and Hebei Provinces. Mao and his headquarters were finally established in Jin, Chahar, and Ji, their liberated region. His followers then consolidated their forces there. Later, on December 30, 1948, Mao gave his historical New Year's message for 1949 to the entire country. In his message, *Carry The Revolution Through to The End*, Mao stated: "the Chinese people would" prevail in "the great war of liberation" and that "even the enemy no longer doubted the outcome." Mao hailed the impending victory of 1949 as the "overthrow of feudal oppression of thousands of years and the imperialist oppression of a hundred years."

The art of writing or solving codes is much more sophisticated and advanced in the modern era than historically. Once Julius Caesar preferred hiding information by a shift of three letters in a plain-text message. Today these simple methods of hiding secrets have been replaced by employing electronic machines or applications of cryptography such as is used in transmitting information on ATM cards or requiring passwords to open files on computers. Encryption and decryption are controlled by algorithms and variable keys. During his time with Mao, Dad relied mostly on the telegraph, radio signals, pen, and paper. His main duty was to send telegraph dispatches in secret codes to the front line troops in the war zones all over the country. Any moves or directions to the Red Army from the headquarters had to be secretly coded and sent to the troops by Dad and his few other colleagues. The job was top security and the army's telecommunication unit had many responsibilities. Though the Red Army and the Nationalist Army had tried to decode each others' signals, for the most part the Red Army's secret codes proved too difficult to be decoded by the Nationalist Army. The technology at that time wasn't advanced. "If we received the enemy's signals, our specialists would try to decode their secret codes. On the other hand, if they successfully decoded our signals, we were long gone," said Dad. It was a cat and mouse game. Since Mao's forty hid out in the vast rural countryside, not in cities, it was difficult for the enemy to find them. Dad's unit worked only in the early mornings or in the middle of the night. By this time Dad had been directly working with Mao for about seven to eight months.

Their living conditions became harsh and more difficult as their food supply dwindled. Even at the outset, food supplies had been at risk, since the villages that they had to rely on were robbed and terrorized constantly by the Nationalist Army. "We only ate porridge made from black bean flour. Before cooking, we got rid of the black bean skins and used the remaining inner beans to make flour. They were delicious to eat in the beginning, but afterwards you felt like your stomach was going to explode and you farted a lot," Dad told me after I asked him about what they ate in such a harsh environment. Even Mao had to eat the same food, no different from the others except that some rice was added to his black bean porridge. As I was listening to Dad, my brain got off track a bit. Did this mean that the great leader, Mao, also farted like the rest of his followers? A being of great stature and extraordinary strength such as Mao should have a desirable quality to contain his emission of gas. At least he should not openly commit this sin of etiquette in front of his fellow men. I suppose when facing humble circumstances such as these, all men were equal. The group of forty consisted of top ranking, key advisors to Mao and his army. Nevertheless, all of them had to line up for the same bowl of black bean porridge. Each of them could only have one bowl, with no refills at each meal. They often had to march on empty stomachs.

The group of forty walked for seven or eight hours, or sometimes even eleven or twelve hours a day, depending on the circumstances at the time. If they learned that their enemy was near, they would hide out in the fields and perhaps sit there for a half day or so until the enemy had passed by. Even if it rained cats and dogs, or was very dismal at night, they still had to walk. Often they couldn't see anything while they were walking during moonless, dark nights. At such times, they would all hold onto a rope grasped tightly as they blindly marched in a line. Dad remembered that he felt that they had to walk endlessly. They were so tired that sometimes they walked while they were sleeping. These were the gloomiest hours just before the dawn.

Once Mao's group of forty had reached the Jin, Chahar, and Ji region, conditions improved immensely. Now they had plenty of rice to eat, which during these hard times was considered a delicacy. Dad and the rest of group were as hungry as wolves the first day they arrived. Their appetites at first were inexhaustible. The more rice the villagers had cooked for them, the more they could eat. "We finished eating every single grain of rice provided, including the grains that were burned on the bottom of the rice pot. You couldn't imagine how hungry we were. We had just walked for eighty or ninety miles and were ravenous for any scrap of food available, no matter how badly cooked or burned," Dad related.

Dad's story reminded me of my own. During my years of laboring in a village in Inner Mongolia, we had little food to eat. We were provided with nothing but the same plain yams day in and day out, at least for the initial months. One would think, especially at that time, that yams would constitute a delicious meal. We started with boiled yams, then switched to baked yams. After one month, we became creative by cutting either boiled or baked yams made available to us and toasting the pieces sliced on top of a heating stove in our multi-purpose bedroom. Following another month of eating the toasted slices, we became even more creative. We would leave sliced yams on a table by a window under the sun indoors for one or two days, until they turned into semi-dried sweet dehydrated slices. In America nowadays, some people replace rawhide with dried sweet potato slices for their larger dogs to enjoy with their powerful jaws. Back then, I initially enjoyed this newly created feast, yet I quickly tired of them, especially when my gums became swollen and sore from the excess chewing on these pieces of rawhide-textured sweet potato. I discovered that my gums began developing pockets where they join the teeth. I am not sure if my pain came from eating too many yams, or from the gum disease or bacteria that lived in my mouth. I know I had no time to wash the food away, or rinse, brush, and keep my teeth clean. Perhaps the lack of nutrition was the key factor. After the first six months, our chef finally enhanced nutrition by adding streamed white bread and Chinese cabbage. By the way, the chef had no formal training in any culinary field. His authority over our cuisine originated solely from his wearing a chef's hat and being assigned the duty for the whole crew, and voila, we had our instant chef! If we were lucky, we got our special treat – a cabbage dish with either horse or camel meat. I had no idea where they got the meat from. I remember that the tasteless camel meat was tough, coarse, and hard to swallow. In terms of the cabbage dish with horse meat, it smelled like urine. I couldn't bear to eat sterile cabbage liquid with a strong odor, so I often dumped it out and abandoned my nutritional enhancement.

Anyway, to return to Dad's march with Mao, many in the group of forty had joined Mao from rural parts of the country and had never been to a bigger town populated by more than a few hundred people before. Some places that they had marched through en route to the Jin, Chahar and, Ji region were more advanced. There they already had electricity, a convenience that some of the marchers had never heard of. Some didn't understand that electricity could generate light. Soon after they had settled down in the Jin, Chahar, and Ji region a joke circulated regarding their unfamiliarity with electricity. During the first night, one fellow in the group wanted to light his cigarette. The room that he was sharing with Dad and a few others had electricity. He was trying to light his cigarette using the one and only light bulb in the room. However, after trying several times he was still unable to convert the light into a spark that would light the cigarette. He became impatient and smashed the bulb to pieces in frustration, plunging the room into darkness for the whole evening until the bulb was replaced the next morning. "We were so barbaric," chuckled Dad at the memory.

Before the summer of 1948 and the liberation of Beijing from the Nationalist army, several other branches of the Red Army joined Mao's group. At this time Dad was stationed in the Pingshan county region in Hebei Province, close to Beijing. Mao and his central government decided to establish a unit reporting directly to the headquarters of Xinhua News Agency in the central region of the country. To re-enforce the new unit with fresh hands, Mao's headquarters sent Dad and five others to join the new central Xinhua unit. After the Mid-Autumn Festival, also called the Moon Festival, of 1948, they set out on their journey. To reach this newly established Xinhua unit was no simple journey. Although some regions of the country along the way were already liberated by the Red Army, they had to pass through the areas that were still in the hands of Nationalist Army. Dad and the five others had to make the necessary adjustments to avoid the enemy, take detours, cross the Yellow River, and pass by the Luoyang area. Finally they arrived at their destination, Yu Xi in Henan Province, where the unit had been initially established. However, after a few months the unit was shifted to Zhengzhou, Henan Province, on the southern bank of the Yellow River and west of Luoyang. Later, in May of 1949, the unit changed its residence one more time to its final destination, in the city of Wu Han in Hubei Province.

As I was listening to the distinctive rhythms of Dad's Shanxi accent on the tape, I wondered if he felt proud that he was chosen to be among this elite combat force by Mao's headquarters. Or perhaps this thought had never crossed his mind. Perhaps he merely had no time to ponder his inclusion among the elite, since he and the rest of the group were persistently chased night and day by their enemy. What a kind of state of mind did Dad have at this stage of his life? Why was he willing to risk his neck to pursue the Nationalists during this brutal civil war? What had motivated him? He must have had a personal goal that was larger than life; he must have had a noble aspiration that stimulated his desire for this pursuit. In following his beliefs and principles, he had undertaken an adventure at his own risk for a greater cause. I wondered what this experience meant to him. Did it have any significant impact on him as a young man then, and as an adult who now had already reached his highest status? He told this remarkable life story at this decisive period of history without further elaborations on his thoughts. It seemed that he only wished to give meaning to his heart.

I wondered if Dad found the meaning of his life through this hardship. I am aware that I am putting myself in danger by asking such a question, since the concept of "meaning of a life" is philosophically complex. Without question, one can reach many different conclusions. Perhaps at that time the purpose of his life was to fight for a better existence for himself and for the entire country, even if it seemed impossible that anyone could endure such hash conditions. The Chinese Civil War was well worth for the fight for him and for the Red Army then. Sixty years after that war, was Dad still searching for the meaning of his life? Did he find the same conclusion? Finding meaning in one's life, perhaps, is like a circle of light that rotates, turns, and constantly makes discovery and re-discovery throughout one's life journey. Once found, when circumstances change, one has to march on and move forward continuously. Searching for meaning in one's being is a lifelong process. However, at this point of time, I am not sure if Dad's life goal has changed. I sensed an exhaustion of Dad's rocket engine during this time spent together. The root of his exhaustion seemed to be expressed in his appearance and manner rather than verbally. He had reached a particular stage in the expected progression of his life. In his own way, Dad had already hiked all the way up to the top of the Yosemite Falls and had even continued the climb to the peak of Mount Everest.

Perhaps it is unrealistic for me to hope for his comeback by trying to rekindle the fire of his youth. On a smaller but parallel scale, my experience in Inner Mongolia during the Cultural Revolution has defined me and had a great impact on me as an American immigrant. This experience has enabled me to endure, to adapt, and to stand up when I fell down. It has taught me to search for the unknown and continuously redefine myself in this new found world. I am not sure if I can avoid falling into the same hole as Dad's current mind-set one day, but for now I have mixed feelings about his sober disposition toward the final stage of his life journey. Nevertheless, I am extremely proud of his role as a brave warrior during his march with Mao.

13. 2008 Olympic Games

On a hot July afternoon in 2001, Dad and I dragged our tired bodies slowly onto the sun baked concrete pavement of the sidewalks in west Beijing. We had just spent four hours with Mom in her hospital and were returning home for the rest of the day. Mom's hospital seemed to be my second home during my visit to Beijing this time. Mom had been there for several weeks and wasn't doing well. I had hoped we could move her home from the hospital for her final days, but Dad thought she would get better care in the hospital. In case of an emergency, it would be safer for her to be near nurses, doctors, and medicine. In his heart, Dad still had a glimmer of hope that one day Mom would become well again. It was hard for him to accept Mom's failing condition. He was pushing Mom's precious life to the limit, and had been encouraging her to keep going. He let everyone in the hospital know that Mom needed to be kept alive as long as possible. It was unthinkable for Dad to see the love of his life gone. Mentally he could not handle it, and was not ready to accept the fact that his partner for fifty years was near the end of her life.

In search of refuge from the searing heat on the street, Dad and I unconsciously added wings to our feet and hastened our pace. Saying nothing, Dad walked briskly with an anxious look on his weathered face. Occasionally I would break the ice by asking him about the new construction along on each side of the street that we were just passing through. The hospital was only few blocks away from home, but today the distance seemed longer. I had walked on the same street many times in my younger years. In the early 1960s and the later 1970s, the houses on this very street were mostly two or three stories, built with bricks, and painted either grey or brown. Most of the buildings had been torn down now and replaced by tall modern concrete structures. The first floor of many newly constructed buildings along the street was occupied by fast food eateries, such as Pizza Hut, Kentucky Fried Chicken, McDonald's, and various Chinese stores or restaurants. My familiar neighborhood had changed drastically in the few years since my last visit there. As a matter of a fact, the whole city itself seemed to be in a construction zone. Wherever I went, I saw new structures that were about to be completed. It was an exciting era in China, but Dad and I were in no mood to discuss political reforms or the Chinese economic revolution.

Every morning when I was home, we would deliver a home-made breakfast to Mom in the hospital, where she had been staying for a few weeks. After Dad had left for home to prepare Mom's lunch, I would stay by her bedside for a few hours, talking to her occasionally, and watching her get poked by needles or IVs by the hospital nurses. I would leave Mom for a brief nap at home once she finished her lunch. Then Dad and I were on the move bringing Mom's dinner to the hospital again. By the end of the day when we finally retired, it was usually close to 9:00 PM. That was our daily routine.

While in the States, I routinely phoned Dad weekly and always checked with him about Mom's health condition.

During my last call to him before this trip to Beijing, Dad sounded different and very quiet. "I think you should come home soon. Your mom is not doing well," Dad said. I sensed the urgency in his tone. Mom's condition must have got worse, I thought. Dad wouldn't urge me to go home right away unless something went very wrong. I booked a plane ticket immediately and left for Beijing a few days after that.

July in Beijing is unbearably hot and humid. The capital is well-known for its humid continental climate. To compound the situation, the mild Mediterranean climate on the Californian coast had spoiled me. I couldn't stand heat like this anymore, nor could I believe this was the place where I grew up. Back then there was no air conditioning either at home or in schools. Now it seemed impossible that anyone could tolerate such extreme heat and humidity without modern conveniences to modify the indoor climate. I wondered how I had managed to previously survive here under this kind of harsh weather. Somehow I was able to endure it in my youth. Perhaps this is the result of global climate change over the past decades. On the other hand, perhaps the climate here has never changed and it is I who have transformed.

The air conditioning on that hot July day couldn't work hard enough to cool down the room, but Dad and I were still glad that we were inside and not out on the street. After completing our third visit to the hospital later that day, it was already after 9:30 PM. Dad and I hadn't yet had supper. We were dog tired. While we were sitting in Dad's dining room eating the leftovers, we suddenly heard a loud explosion outside. It was followed with huge lights that brightened the dark sky. Dad and I quietly gazed at each other; neither of us felt like standing up to find out what was going on. The sound of explosions outside became increasingly louder and louder. I finally gave in and rushed to the backyard. There was a huge smoky cloud slowly drifting across the brightened sky. Another explosion followed right above my head, away up in the sky, as I was stepping outside. Looking straight up, I saw a series upon series of spectacular explosions of huge, bright, and beautiful fireworks.

"Look, there are fireworks," I shouted at Dad through. the screen door excitedly. Dad was still sitting on his chair in the dining room. He didn't move an inch.

"Oh, it must be about the Olympic Games. Beijing must have been chosen to be the host of 2008 Olympic Games," Dad responded me, emotionless.

"This is big news for China, Dad. Come to see the fireworks with me," I yelled back at him eagerly.

"I don't want to see it today. I am too tired," Dad said simply.

The reverberations of music mixed with loud firework pops and screams had invaded the entire neighborhood. Judging from the intensity of the sounds, the fireworks must be from somewhere nearby. They must have been shot up into the sky from the tall buildings behind our house. I turned around and looked at Dad again. He was still sitting on the same chair in the same position. He seemed to slip into deep, distant thoughts. As I recalled, Dad had always loved fireworks, especially during the holidays and special national events, but tonight he was not bursting with joy and excitement as before. For a second I tried to examine his face and read his mind, but couldn't figure out what he was thinking. Perhaps he was thinking about Mom, who was an avid sports fan and would love to watch the Olympic Games. If Mom were with us here tonight, she surely would have enjoyed this historic moment very much. Like popped bubbles, Dad's hope had evaporated. Mom was lying on the hospital bed by herself.

Though I was afraid of the sound of explosions in my youth, I now loved fireworks. Any pyrotechnical exhibitions always made me feel happier. Attending annual firework showcases at Tian An Men Square on October 1st during the evening celebrations of Chinese National Day were big events for my family when I was growing up. Dad loved the crowds at these magnificent social occasions. As he would watch the displays, his typically calm voice instantly changed into loud, excited high-pitched squeals. He would point a finger to the sky as he shouted enthusiastically in appreciation. Like the fluttering wings of a butterfly, his arms would move up and down constantly. While in the States, the only great pyro-technics display I witnessed that could be remotely compared to the ones I saw at Tan An Men Square was the event that I attended in Detroit, Michigan, many years ago. Across the international boundary, the Detroit display was coordinated by the American and Canadian governments to combine each national celebration of 4th of July and 1st of July respectively. That firework showcase was indeed grand. After moving to the west coast, I attended a few local 4th of July celebrations, which had only relatively small firework displays. While Dad was staying with me in the States, one July 4th I took him to our local town celebration to witness a small firework display. He agreed to go along, but told me afterwards, "China has much better and bigger fireworks. There is nothing compara-ble to see here." Although he had several opportunities, Dad never went with me and watched another firework show in the U.S. again after that. He preferred to stay at home alone.

Here I was, standing in Dad's backyard on the other side of the Pacific Ocean alone, looking at the dark sky, beautifully ornamented by the bright lights followed by swirling, smoky clouds. For a second I couldn't believe the display was right here in my childhood neighborhood. These events had never happened this close when I was a child. In the past we had to make an effort to travel a couple of hours to observe firework displays. The Chinese government is well known in the world for putting on beautiful and dramatic firework showcases. After all, ancient China invented fireworks. That summer night, it turned out, was just the beginning of a lasting celebration. To the people and government of China, hosting the 2008 Olympic Games was the culmination of years of effort and anticipation, a monumental symbol of the arrival a new China alongside the many western countries who had played host in past years. China was no longer a weak, sick, or crippled country. China was at long last able to stand tall, strong, and proud in front of the other great nations of the world. That summer night, however, Dad showed no interest in celebrating this historic moment with me and with the entire capital city of China. Looking into the sky that flashed and blazed with dozens of colors, my enthusiasm gradually cooled down as the drifting clouds of smoke marked the finality of the display. Had I been attached to a mood gauging device, it would have crashed to a reading of zero. I woke up abruptly from the sparkling glory into reality. I went inside and Dad had already disappeared from the dining room. He had already gone to bed without saying good night. I went to bed, the popping of firecrackers like machine gun bursts outside didn't even bother me and I quickly fell asleep. That was July 13, 2001.

Early next morning, I learned from the local TV news that after two rounds of voting by the members of the International Olympic Committee (IOC), Beijing had been awarded the Games by an absolute majority of votes over four competitors. The Games would take place in Beijing from August 8 to August 24, 2008. It would be only the third time that the Summer Games had been held in Asia. Dad and I quickly finished breakfast, turned off the TV, and left home for the hospital to visit Mom. I had been staying in Beijing with Dad and Mom for three weeks now. Today was the last day before my scheduled flight for San Francisco from the Beijing international airport early next morning. The hardest part of this trip had finally arrived; I would have to say good-bye to Mom.

When Dad and I arrived at the hospital, Mom was lying on the bed motionless with her eyes shut. I couldn't tell if she was asleep. Once full of life, Mom in recent months had now lost much of her mobility. She had gone blind a few years before. Her physical disability didn't seem to affect her brain function and speech ability. She was alert, her mind was still as sharp as ever, and she always spoke clearly with authority. I sat down on a chair at Mom's bedside and reached out my hand to hers, holding it gently. I examined her face for a moment, trying to see similarities with my facial features. As a child I was told that my face resembled the faces of both Dad and Mom. If my face were divided it into two parts, I looked a lot like Dad from the nose up, and had Mom's mouth and other features from the nose down. My nose was a toss-up. Sometimes it resembled Dad's, other times it resembled Mom's. Mom was out-going, warm, and beautiful, while Dad was always kind, patient, and considerate. However, I don't have Mom's beauty, nor do I have Dad's patience. In that sense, I only partially resemble my parents.

After years of poor health, Mom's face wasn't weathered with wrinkles; her skin was still smooth and beautiful at the age of seventy. "You are here now," Mom quietly acknowledged me being with her. I told her about the news of Olympic Games and the firework shows. She didn't say a word; her eyes were still closed. Her mouth opened slightly with a tiny grin. As I gazed at her face, I wondered if it was too difficult for Mom to learn about the news I had just shared with her. Mom was athlete in her better years. Contrary to gender stereotypes, it was Dad who had never got tired of shopping and it was Mom who always loved sports. Was Mom thinking about the news? Perhaps she was saying to herself that she wouldn't be alive to listen to all of the media broadcasts about the Summer Games when it finally came to Beijing in seven years. The rest of the morning I refrained from mentioning the Summer Games again. I didn't wish to disturb Mom further.

For a few hours that morning, I was sitting beside Mom while holding and rubbing her hands. We remained silent for the most of the time. All of the guidance Mom had given me in my youth floated into my mind as I was staring at her motionless face. What a fool I was not to take her advice seriously. As a teen I often felt suffocated by her admonitions to me and thought we were not able to share and understand each other's thoughts and feelings on a deep level. Her valuable instruction could not prevent me from rebelling against her. I was hot under the collar and banging my head against whatever she said. Mom once told me soulfully after we had a verbal confrontation, "You don't understand. As a mother, you are constantly worrying yourself sick over your child. You are in great pain if your child runs into trouble." Only decades later, as a mother myself, could I sincerely comprehend the richness of her meaningful statement. I wanted to tell her how sorry I was at this point, but invoked only a silent wish instead. Without saying it, I knew our hearts and minds were finally linked together. Occasionally Mom woke me up as I was deep in my own thoughts. She would randomly ask me questions about Mao Mao and Celine, her two grandchildren. She then requested me to promise that I would never forget about my birth country. "Keep in touch with your brother and Mao Mao," Mom said softly and clearly. During these hours, Dad mostly sat in the corner of the room observing us silently.

"Wei, you are leaving tomorrow. You should go home to finish packing," Dad finally broke his sullen silence.

"You go. Please go now," Mom replied calmly and emotionlessly.

"It's okay. I can stay here a little longer," I said, hesitating to face the moment of saying good-bye. Perhaps it would be my last time, I thought.

"You go. Go now," Mom responded to me firmly.

This time, the tone of Mom's voice seemed to be different. The moment of truth, the moment that I had been afraid of, had arrived. My throat was tight; my mouth was dry. I was apprehensive. From head to toe, my anxiety took over my whole body. Dad stood up pacing back and forth in the room, then stepped outside. Mom and I were now alone. I stood up, cleared my throat and said to her, "I need to buy few things and finish my packing before my flight tomorrow morning. It is time for me to go, Mom."

"We will never see each other again," Mom said simply and softly without moving her body.

"Yes. We will see each other again. I will always see you in my heart," I said determinedly while holding my tears.

My throat seemed to tighten up even further and tears flooded my eyes, running down to my cheeks uncontrollably. Sorrow and sadness overpowered me. I wanted to burst into tears and cry out loud. But at that very moment, my conscience told me to control myself, to hold my unstoppable streams. I didn't wish Mom to hear me crying. It was the last thing that I wished Mom to find out. I felt such an urge to reach out to her heart and hoped that, in the depths of her soul, she knew that there was no ending to spiritual life that would be continuing in another world. Mom's spirit will always be present in my body and soul as long as I live. I leaned down and gave her a long and tender kiss on her forehead. An overflow of tears came down from my eyes like a stream. Holding them back without making any vibrations, I turned my back around immediately and left the room quietly. My heart was fractured into many pieces. The tears pumping from my eyes couldn't numb the tissues of my brain. I broke down and sobbed like a baby all the way home. Saying nothing, Dad followed me. What could he say to me? Nothing could be said that would comfort us. Nothing. As it turned out, this was the last time I was able to talk to Mom. I wasn't able to rush back in time from the States to see her one more time before she passed away three months after this visit.

Back in the States there was plenty of news about awarding China the host country of the 2008 Summer Olympic Games. The choice of Beijing was a subject of criticism by many western media. Some politicians and special interest groups were concerned about air pollution in Beijing and the country's human rights record. The Chinese government, on the other hand, warned against the politicizing of the Olympics by some western countries, while promoting the Games aggressively and investing heavily in new facilities, infrastructure, and transportation systems. Under normal circumstances, I am impartial when it comes to sports competitions. I am almost completely oblivious to the fortunes of our regional teams and to the fact that the San Francisco Giants won the World Series in 2010, and that the San Jose Sharks won the western NHL division title in the same year. Yes, oblivious. That is, with the exception of the Olympic Games. Every four years, I faithfully watch the Olympics on TV, regardless of where the Games are held. I regard them in a different light than other sports events. The Olympics symbolize world peace, harmony, and human spirit. Unfortunately, the Games are often mixed up with politics and used by governments and special interest groups to stage their interests and ply their points of view.

Dad visited Beijing again in fall of 2007. Before leaving California that year, he promised to return in the spring of 2008. He would have to give up a lot to be back with me in the States, I thought. "Sorry, Dad. You will have to miss the Olympic Games in Beijing," I said to him. "It is okay. I can watch the Games on TV." Dad knew I needed him to be with Celine in the summer of 2008 while Terry and I were at work during the day. Someone had to look after her between her school breaks and summer programs. Terry and I were too busy to provide the kind of attention that we thought Celine deserved to have at home. I always admire single parents who can do it all, juggling career, kids, and home life at the same time. How do they do it? They must be super human beings. I have given up trying to be a super woman ever since giving birth to Celine. My career was going well and it was too soon to retire from my job. Dad could lend me a helping hand and solve my problem.

When August 8, 2008, had finally arrived, I could feel an unspeakable excitement around me. Even the air smelled different. Dad and I skipped our daily walk after supper. We were ready for the major historic event – the opening ceremony of the 2008 Olympic Games to be broadcast live on NBC in just thirty minutes. Mentally we had prepared for this moment for a long time. I still couldn't believe it was finally here. This was not any Summer Games; it was the Beijing Olympic Games. Frankly I had no idea what to expect tonight. As I was watching the pounding drums, dancers with ancient costumes, children singing on the center stage of the National Stadium, and bright and colorful pyrotechnics exploding above the stadium in the sky, I realized something significant had just happened on the TV screen. The performances at the opening ceremony touched me. I felt proud to be a Chinese American and found a new fountain of life. For half of my life I have worked and lived in America. I am now so used to the way of life and feel comfortable being a part of the culture here. Nevertheless, no matter how "white" I am perceived to be on the surface, deep down in my heart, for the first time in a long time, I have never felt so sure that a part of me still belongs to the more familiar, ancient culture there where I grew up, and in which basic concepts were molded. I have been struggling with the contrasts of human mental impressions from both continents ever since I landed here. Nevertheless, perceptions are only skin-deep; they have limits and can be challenged. Ideally, no one should be perceived differently on the basis of their appearance, but should be judged on the quality of their character. Beyond a thin outer layer, all people are equal. To try to adapt to a foreign cultural environment and to try to "do in Rome as the Romans do" does not mean one forgets about his or her own roots. These are survival strategies that many before me have adopted, modified, and found success in this unaccustomed Earth. Sitting in front of the TV, watching those magnificent performances in their glory, I realized that I had never thought about myself differently, but as a Chinese American. I had never stopped believing in keeping my own identity, being a person of absolute integrity, and staying true to my core values. If I were perceived differently, so be it. I knew who I was and what I stood for. Until that day, I had never been so proud of my country of origin.

During the next two weeks I was glued to the TV screen watching the Olympic Games every night, often hearing Dad from his room across the hall shouting the results, with his comments, about a specific event. We cheered excitedly for the Chinese athletes who had just won a gold medal. By the closing celebration of the Beijing 2008 Olympic Games, Chinese athletes had walked away with fifty-one gold medals and one hundred medals altogether. A total of 11,028 athletes from all over world had participated in the Games. The 2008 Summer Games had reached the largest television audience in Olympic history. A "truly exceptional Games" was declared by the president of International Olympic Committee (IOC) at the closing ceremony in Beijing. The 2008 Summer Olympic Games were a source of national pride for China and for all Chinese overseas. I wondered if Mom was watching the Games with me and Dad in heaven. Knowing her pride, I am sure she must be very pleased. I could hear her saying, "Well done. Well done, China!"

14. East or West, Which is Best?

Dad in Colorado

After only a few months of being in California after his Beijing visit in 2008, Dad started getting restless again. He would like to go back to China in September, he told me. This was to become his particular pattern of behavior each year after coming back from China each spring.

"You have just received your immigration status. Why don't you stay here for a while? My home is yours. This is your home now, Dad," I said to him sincerely.

"I have a home in China too. Your brother and my grandson are there. I can't help thinking of them."

"How about a short visit. You can stay there for six months and come back to us next year. You will like it here eventually, Dad. Could you promise me to return to us in the spring of next year?"

"I will think about it."

Dad had the whole thing planned out. In my mind, I wanted to convince him to stay with me in the States permanently. He would feel more comfortable being here after a few years of adjustment, I thought. It was only matter of time; he would get used to it eventually. After all, I got used to it. Dad told me he didn't want to be my responsibility. "You have Celine to worry about," he said. Often Celine had to stay late at her after-school care after many of her friends there had already been picked up. As a Mom, it hurt me to think that I wasn't able to spend more time with my child. I wished Dad could help me out with Celine by being here. However, from time to time I wondered what a kind of help Dad could really offer me. I needed a driver for Celine, but Dad couldn't drive. Bless his heart, Dad wanted to prepare supper for us, but Celine didn't like his cooking. I needed someone to play with Celine. Dad tried, but soon Celine lost interest playing with him. Celine would like someone to talk to, but Dad couldn't speak English and sign language could only go so far between them. Selfishly I wished Dad could help me more, but I was also aware that there was a limit. I knew to be here Dad had added one more responsibility on my shoulders, yet

I didn't want to openly admit it. Whenever Dad said, "I have added a lot of trouble to you by being here," I retorted, "No trouble at all, Dad." I didn't wish to hurt Dad's feelings. We both knew I wasn't telling the truth. My feelings about Dad's stay were complex. I wished to spend more time with him, especially since he was nearing the end of life's long journey. I felt guilty that I wasn't able to be more helpful to Dad when he was Mom's caregiver. I wasn't on the front line when he needed me the most. Physiologically and emotionally, I really wanted to feel his presence and to have him be here with me. Was I being too selfish?

Our hillside house is surrounded by tranquility. I wondered if Dad missed the excitement of big city life. "I like to be quiet. I don't like crowds," Dad said whenever I asked him. In truth, perhaps he was more than a little isolated. Trying to make me feel better, Dad told me that every day he caught up on current events by watching the Chinese news on the San Francisco Channel 26 TV station. In that way he could keep himself connected to the other side of the Pacific Ocean and the outside world. He entertained himself when we were away by reading the Chinese books that I had borrowed for him. There weren't many Chinese on this side of the hill. We would grab every single opportunity to party with my Chinese friends over the hill so that Dad would have someone similar to talk to, if for only just for a few hours. In so doing, he might feel better connected to his roots.

Food was exceptional at the Chinese get-togethers over the hill. The varieties of mouthwatering Chinese food presented at the parties were always delicious and colorful, and could make one feel very homesick just by looking at them. "My home cooking is the best. You can't get it anywhere in America," one cheerful and straightforward host pronounced proudly. Her signature food was pan-fried Chinese pancakes, which apparently had developed into the main chat topic, monopolizing her dinner table conversation at the party. To showcase how skillful she was, before the meal she first prepared a soft dough using wheat flour in front of all her guests. On a floured work surface, she magically rolled a piece of dough out into a thin square. Then she sprinkled some chopped green onions onto the dough evenly, rolled the dough up into a rope shape, and later into a flat spiral shape. Then she gently rolled it out into a pancake with some green onions and pre-marinated ground beef folded inside. To finish off her work of art, she pan-fried each pancake in a hot skillet until it turned golden brown on both sides. She finally cut the first ready-to-eat pancake into several pieces for the enthusiastic cheerleaders watching by the stove. The host wouldn't be satisfied until she heard people say, "Wonderful pancake! Great chef!" I had, on occasion, seen these pancakes on display at various Asian markets over the hill, but since I was not a regular visitor to these places, I rarely had a chance to taste one. Therefore I had to put all doubts aside and simply choose to believe that my friend's homemade pancake was indeed la crème de la crème.

These friends of mine have always cooked Chinese food at home regardless how many years they have been in the States. "Western food doesn't taste good. I am not used to it," another party host declared. Their allegiance to Chinese food makes me feel like an oddball among them. I normally go to Nob Hill to get my groceries, while my friends always shop at their local Asian markets. I like Chinese food, but also enjoy other types of cuisine. They only eat Chinese. I grew up with these people, so we often talk about the past events that we had shared in China decades ago, yet we really don't seem to know anything about each other anymore. They don't have a clue about how my life is and what I have been going through in America and vice versa. Our tie to the past seems to be more than enough for us to be securely bonded with one and another on this foreign land which we now call home. A thin string of common background in the past attaches us together. Today we no longer seem to have much in common, but because of that common background from our youth, these Chinese friends have unconditionally accepted me, even though I am culturally too white for them and have married a "white ghost". They have also received my "white ghost" as adequate, maybe because he speaks Chinese.

Dad naturally fit in right away at these get-togethers and felt a sense of ease, while I often felt lost, especially in situations such as when there was a lively discussion about a specific drama show on the local Chinese TV station. Dad understood the drama plots that I had never watched and knew the biographical information on specific Chinese movie or TV stars that I had never heard of. He became extremely animated if debating any current affairs regarding the U.S. and China. These exchanges were often emotional and loud, with much shouting in each other's faces in colloquial Chinese across the dinner table. Some at the party have never mastered the English language, no matter how long they have been in the States, even those that have been here for more than twenty years. They have been living in a segregated life of their choosing. The concept of "melting pot" is still strongly associated with the American culture and its identity. Though some have melted half way, many have never melted at all. According to my Chinese friends, my cooking isn't up to their standard. My summer BBQ and winter hot pot (Chinese fondue) at my house are nothing in comparison to theirs. The travel distance between my house and theirs doesn't help the situation either. They aren't eager to take a trip to my direction, even after I have sent them a sincere invitation. "You live too far. It is too difficult to drive to your place," one friend frankly declined my invitation. By contrast, our response to their invitations is simple. We didn't mind driving over the hill; that was always a special treat for Dad and us.

Dad's tape recorder that we bought for him to learn English had mysteriously disappeared from his desk shortly after he first arrived in America in 2004. Later discovered residing in his bedroom closet, it has remained there ever since.

"How come you stopped learning English? You are going to live here. It's important to understand at least a few important words and sentences," I said to Dad during one of our daily walks.

"Em, em…"

"Why don't you teach Celine a Chinese word and she teach you an English word each day," I suggested to him once again.

"Okay, okay."

Dad and Celine exchanged their lessons a few times at the dinner table. Shortly thereafter, their cross training sessions ceased unless I pushed them further. Obviously there was no motivation from either side. Alas, it turned out that in his mind Dad had never planned to remain in the States as I originally hoped. He had no intention of staying here permanently perhaps, even when he was first granted a Green Card at the San Francisco airport in 2004. During the past five years, Dad would stay with me for six months and insisted on visiting Beijing for the other half year. He had plenty of reasons why he needed to go back and forth so often. Besides missing his grandson and son in Beijing, what was going to be his next justification? I naively believed that he would eventually tire of traveling and would stay in America once these trips wore him out. I was half right: he did eventually tire of the frequent jet trips over the Pacific. However, as the years went by, the number of months that he stayed here grew fewer and fewer. Of course, the time he spent across the Pacific Ocean got longer and longer.

"I won't be back again next year." Dad finally pulled the trigger one summer night as we were pacing slowly on the neighborhood road.

"Why? You don't want to lose your Green Card, do you?" I said, reminding him that if he ceased staying in America, his Green Card could be invalided.

"I haven't visited my birthplace for about sixty years. I wish to go back one more time before I no longer can move."

"Why don't you come back here for one more year, Dad?"

"I am getting old. I don't want to travel anymore."

"You feel old if you think you are. It all depends on your own mindset."

This was the same old debate on aging repeated between Dad and me so many times before. The arguments always seemed to teeter somewhere on the brink between reason and emotion.

Beneath his frequent excuses related to the limitations imposed by aging, I wondered what the real reason was that led to Dad's final blow. Though the living standard in China has improved dramatically over the past decade, it is still at its infancy compared with that of America or other developed countries. I had provided everything that I could for Dad, but it didn't seem to be enough for him. Why couldn't I convince him to stay? Was it because of the different cultural environment here? Or could it be that he could never find in our small California community the smells, tastes, friendships, and the hustle and bustle that he had grew up in and become accustomed to while living in the teeming cities of China? "Different strokes for different folks." I found myself repeating the same phrase again. But I was a part of the close family, his flesh and blood. Was I not good enough to induce him to stay? Dad had never truly settled down in the States. Was this country only a rest stop for him? Obviously Dad was longing for something more, something more than just being and living with me. What was that something? This time Dad was determined not to return to the U.S. ever again. An old saying flashed in my mind, "East and West, Home is the best." In Dad's mind, his home would always be China, which offered him the best of everything. Why didn't I see that? Still, I felt blindsided.

On his personal journey, Dad had struggled and endured all his life. His generation was unfortunately caught amidst many uprisings, wars, and revolutions. He was in the middle of the political crises when China was in its turmoil. He had suffered the loss of his parents as a child. He was criticized for being a capitalist during the Cultural Revolution because once he bought poultry to feed his family. He had lost his position, was dragged outside his office building by the Red Guards, and was forced to parade on the streets wearing a sign saying, "I am an anti-revolutionist." Many years after those heartbreaking events, ironically there is no hatred in Dad, but only love of his country and his party. Why is he still so attached to China after all that suffering? Why is China still the best place for him? Many people would almost die for a Green Card. Many of Dad's friends of his generation have immigrated to America and stayed for good. Why couldn't he do the same?

One night, back home from our walk, I found Dad drinking his favorite Jasmine tea and resting in his chair in his bedroom. I went in and sat down on his bed getting myself comfortable. I had brought a tape recorder with me as I had done every night this summer, the summer of 2008. I had a lot of questions for Dad and wanted to keep the recorder running.

"Dad, how has your life in China been after your retirement?"

"I retired in 1990. After that I used all my free time looking after your mom and taking her to hospitals," Dad said slowly and thoughtfully while sipping tea.

Those years that Dad had talked about seemed to go by so fast, leaving only a fuzzy memory in my mind now. I remembered in the early 1990s that I was stressed out, as I was learning the ropes and struggling in my new work environment. Trying to get used to the institutional politics was more difficult than gaining skills needed for my new job. As a care-free college student for many years in this country, all of sudden I felt I was treated differently, like a competitor species, looking for a niche within a complex ecosystem. I didn't fit in at first and had tangled. Later I recovered, stood up, held my head high along the way, and triumphed in the end.

By 2001, reports of Mom's health went from bad to worse each time I phoned Dad. As my mind was sidetracked on these details in the past, Dad took another sip from the tea cup, then put it down on the table by his chair.

"Before my retirement, I was passed over many times when it was time for a promotion or a salary increase. During the

Cultural Revolution, everything was shut down. I was sent to do manual labor in the countryside in Shanxi Province."

I recalled that while Dad was in Shanxi, I was working on a farm in Inner Mongolia. I didn't know that my brother, who was twelve years old, was in prison during that time. Because of her poor health, Mom was allowed to stay home alone, refusing the request by the Red Guards to join Dad in the countryside. I didn't find out about my brother's situation until I got a letter one day. Inside the envelope I found a hand-written letter from Mom addressed to Dad. This letter should actually have gone to Dad. Mom had accidentally stuck the letter in a wrong envelope and sent it to me instead. My parents didn't want to tell me what had happened to my brother. They were afraid the bad news would interfere with my life on the farm. I have never learned why he was in jail. Whenever I asked, my parents would give their scalps a good scratch and couldn't come up with a convincing answer for me. Any discussions regarding my brother's unfortunate confinement would silence a family gathering.

While my thoughts were elsewhere, Dad cleared his throat, raised his voice, and said, "Later there was a salary reform in the agency where I was working. Due to some internal politics, I was passed over again. Since I had joined the Red Army before 1949, according to our retirement policy I would get my full salary and full medical benefits after I retired. Once in a while I would receive some bonuses during the national holidays or occasionally at certain special events. However, after retiring I have never received any cost of living adjustments. Beijing is getting more expensive over the years. In fact, it is one of the most expensive cities in the country to live in. Currently there is talk about the possibility of salary and pension reform at the agency. Frankly I think an opportunity for us to get a cost of living increase soon is unrealistic."

There is no real pension system at Dad's agency or at the most working places in China. According to a recently circulating story, a new reform is supposed to take place soon. In spite of the new buzz about reforming the Chinese pension and salary system, the process has been painfully slow and its outcome still remains to be seen. Most likely Dad's generation, now approaching their eighties, will not be able to reap the final results of the reform before they die.

"Dad, you have followed the Communist Party ever since you were twelve. What do you think of your entire life up to this point? What are the benefits you have gained by following the Party?" I asked next.

"I lost both of my parents at very young age. Due to my harsh living environment, I had no other choice but to join the Red Army, where I got my education. I was happy in the Red Army, especially when I heard that we won the war against the Japanese and later the Nationalists. It was big news for the entire country. However, afterwards life was still hard at my home in the village. In the army, life was easy. At least there was food on the table, I had clothes to wear, and I got educated there. After the establishment of the People's Republic of China in 1949, you and your brother were born and our life was relatively stable and agreeable before 1954. Though your mom and I were introduced to each other by a common friend and had no previous knowledge of each other, we had a very good marriage for fifty years. We were meant for each other. We promised each other that if one of us got sick down the road, no matter what else happened, the other would be the caregiver till the end. Before your mom passed away, she told me that she had given me too much trouble in my life. We talked often during the last few days of her life."

Later I found out that Mom had encouraged Dad to find another partner once she was gone, but Dad said to her jokingly that he would, if he were in his twenties or thirties. "No one wants me anymore. I am too old," Dad told Mom. After Mom passed away, Dad wished to buy a plot beside Mom's grave so that one day he could be buried alongside her in the same cemetery. In order to give him peace of mind, I contributed some money towards completing his desire.

"Though I had struggles, my personal life was happy regardless of your mom's health. We had survived the Cultural Revolution together. After your mom's passing, I was named the best husband and the best family man by the neighborhood community," Dad went on proudly.

I wonder if the notion of "best" depends on who defines it. A story always has two sides, or has different ways to narrate. Before asking Dad these questions, I had wished, in the end, that I would be satisfied with all his answers. I have to admit I felt somewhat disappointed. His answers to my questions weren't philosophically complex. In my mind, the bottom line of his responses, perhaps, wasn't sophisticated and deep enough either. I hoped for some dramatic statements from him, but all I got was a wish for a simple life, food on the table, clothes to wear, a good family, and a stable living environment. After those years of struggling, he still insisted that China was the best place for him to be. His conclusion was beyond my comprehension, but obvious to Dad. The Red Army had provided a shelter for him when he needed it most. A good marriage to Mom formed a solid foundation rooted deeply in his heart. China is the place where he was born, where he had struggled, where he was triumphant, and where his core beliefs and values originated. China is Dad's home; it always is. It is, indeed, the best place for him. What further answers do I expect from him? He had just expressed profound truths in simple language. Perhaps simple is more. His simple desire and wishes, perhaps, represent basic human instinct after all. I should feel good about his answers.

The concept of home is quite different to me, on the other hand. Born in China, I had also experienced the Cultural Revolution and had survived in a labor camp in Inner Mongolia in my youth. In my adulthood, I had strived to achieve, struggled in higher education, and have succeeded in America. I have gradually found a home in this land of a great opportunity. "East and west. Home is the best." I can now finally and comfortably say that America is my home.

15. Going Home

Dad at the airport

Early September in the central coastal mountain region of California is beautiful. It is a not-so-well-kept secret that once the hordes of vacationers return to their abodes, the locals are left in peace and harmony to enjoy the magnificent weather and gentle transition to fall. The forests are radiant in autumn colors. The local climate can deliver an Indian Summer and the air temperature can rise to over 90°F for a few days. However, for the most part during this time, the coastal clouds start rolling in and the temperature cools down to a comfortable 75°F by 7:00 PM. While the sky was still bright and sunny, Dad and I paced slowly up and then down the narrow neighborhood lane. The sunlight was beaming through the redwood trees that stood tall and straight on each side of the road, providing halo effects on the edges of the sienna bark. Although they are evergreen trees, the dry leaves of the redwoods had started falling; the leaves of the neighborhood's big maple trees had already turned red and yellow. The smell in the air that distinguished fall from summer seemed to arrive here again so soon without notice.

Yesterday I helped Dad pack for his trip to Beijing. His suitcase was too small to fit his gifts, let alone all his belongings. For each additional trip he took, his suitcase grew bigger and bigger. This time was no exception. Once again he needed a bigger suitcase, so we bought another huge one at Ross. Today I prepared rice and stir-fried vegetables for dinner. It was Dad's last supper before leaving for China. Very soon he would be able to enjoy genuine Chinese cuisine in the company of his relatives and friends.

On our last stroll through the redwoods, Dad was walking slowly and silently while I was soaked in random thoughts that had been locked in my mind for a long time. In the past Dad had reminded me several times that this was to be his last year staying here with us in America. However, in my mind I still hoped that he would have a change of heart and return again to stay next year. I wished he would be coming and going like he did many times before. I didn't want to believe this was his last visit. I was so used to having him around every spring and summer since 2004. I was so used to renewing my Chinese language skills with Dad since it was the only language he knew. Celine had grown older and a little wiser. She had refused to learn Chinese a few years before, but recently she had expressed a desire to learn the language. With her grandpa here, she now had absorbed bits and pieces of Chinese language through osmosis in the process of hearing it from us. Although it was still a challenge, she was still hoping to improve her speaking and comprehension next year with Grandpa.

Dad kept charging slowly ahead. Breaking the silence, I made my last plea. "Dad, you should come back for one more year, just one more year. If you wish, you can stop coming when you reach eighty. You are only seventy-eight this year." Looking straight ahead into the sun's rays beaming down through the redwood trees on the roadside, Dad stopped to rest for a few seconds. Taking a deep breath, he went on, giving me the same answer. "No, I can't come back any more. I'd like to visit my home town in Shanxi one more time before I can no longer move around. You see, I haven't visited there for about sixty years." We kept walking silently down the hill. It was quiet enough to be able to hear the sounds of leaves rustling on the trees and birds singing far away. I didn't say anything more after this last request. What more could be said? Dad had firmly made his mind up. He had his mission and he had determined his path.

I was restless without getting much sleep that night. In a few hours we were going to wake up and take Dad to the San Francisco airport one last time. This was going to be the last time his footsteps would tread on American soil. I wound in and out of my dreams and followed random thoughts during the night. The past five years had flown by at laser speed. I didn't realize until now that these years would count as the most important and meaningful years of my life. At a personal level, I had gotten to know and learn more about Dad. We had walked for so many miles together on the neighborhood road after supper each day. These walks had enabled me to bond with him, an opportunity I had missed in my youth in China due to a variety of factors, but mainly because of political upheaval.

Many dramatic domestic and global events had taken place during these five short years. An enormous tsunami had devastated the seaboard of south Asia killing 200,000 people, while the western civilization was celebrating a Christmas holiday season on December 26, 2004. The first Hispanic mayor of Los Angeles was elected in California in 2005, which was a triumph reflecting the state's growing Hispanic population and strong political influence in America. In August of the same year, powerful hurricane Katrina forcibly hit the Gulf Coast near the estuary of the Mississippi River. Two of New Orleans' levees broke and flooded the city. As a result, many in the city were trapped and over one million people were displaced. In 2006 the U.S. Supreme Court admonished the Bush Administration's position that the government could hold suspected terrorists "without due process and without the protection of the Geneva Accords." In 2007 a study by a group of several top scientists on climate change convened by the United Nations announced for the first time that "global warming is 'unequivocal' and that human activity is the main driver, 'very likely' causing most of the rise in temperatures...unless immediate and drastic action were taken, the world was in for centuries of climbing temperatures, rising seas and shifting weather patterns — unavoidable results of the buildup of heat-trapping gases in the atmosphere." The top scientists also predicted that poor regions would be extremely susceptible. Senator Barak Obama became the first African American Democratic Nominee for President on June 3, 2008. On August 8, Beijing became the first Chinese host of the Summer Olympic Games and triumphantly greeted the world.

The whole universe seemed to be in continual flux and evolution during the past five years. Yet everything on the surface around me remained calm and steady. Going beyond the surface and underneath the stillness, Dad and I tried to fill in the gaps and details of past events that we both had missed. During our daily discussions, we had searched for meaning in our lives. We each ended up with a distinct conclusion about the significance of existence of our individual lives. This great land has provided enormous opportunities to the people before me and a bright future to many new immigrants ahead. Many have already succeeded, some have failed, and a few have turned around to go back to their place of origin.

Two centuries ago, the early pioneers in America found themselves isolated in their harsh lives on the prairie. The challenging and unfamiliar environment proved unbearable for many. In the twentieth century of materialistic, modern American society, the essentials of life are conveniently available for most. Dad could live easily and comfortably until the end of his life's journey here with me, but his choice was not to stay in America. Dad's definition of comfort is vastly different from mine. Although recent migrants to America have made the most of this opportunity and embraced this robust society, other people of "delicate sensibility", like Dad, have found life in this alien world to be unbearable. The forces of his nature and his cultural roots are more powerful than the attraction of this new land of freedom. His comfort in China stems from the rich and familiar collective resources of culture, customs, arts, social institutions, and achievements in the Far East. In America he has stubbornly rejected anything new and has refused to learn English. The new wave of immigration from China to America has meant nothing to Dad. He was getting old and didn't wish to be buried in foreign soil. Sadly he didn't see too much future in front of him, whether in America or China. To Dad it was a good visit in America, but it was about time to return home. He was looking forward to a new beginning in China.

As for me, this land has provided a new opportunity in my life, unavailable in China. When I arrived in America about thirty years ago, I was ready for change and eager to turn over a new leaf. In order to take advantage of the opportunities presented, I was willing to do in Rome as the Romans do, willing to accept any challenges that this society might throw at me. In spite of this willingness to adapt, I have never forgotten my roots and my core values. Holding onto these principles to the core and knowing my own identity deep in my heart are essential. Without them I am not able to face my fears, loneliness, and hardships. I enthusiastically draw inspiration from this land of great opportunity, this country's people of astonishing energy, and have embraced the consequences and rewards wholeheartedly. Dad and I have chosen different paths like many pioneers before us. I have found my life in America. My destiny is here.

It was early on the first Saturday morning of September 2008. Terry had already got up, imbibed his ritual cup of coffee, and was busy lugging Dad's heavy suitcases into the trunk of our Camry. Tired after a sleepless night, I made myself a cup of coffee, hoping the caffeine could get me going. After a simple breakfast, we departed for the San Francisco airport on the route through Silicon Valley and over the oak savannas of the Bay Area mountains. The sky was still blanketed with a dense, gray coastal fog as we wended our way on the mountain highway. No one in the car talked and my mind was rewinding the summer events and pondering the significance of this final trip with Dad. Terry was focused on driving while Celine fell asleep. Dad sat motionlessly on the passenger side of the front seat. By the time we had reached the airport, the morning fog was lifting. At the United Airline check-in counter, we were informed that Dad's luggage was overweight and we would have to pay excess baggage fees. After quickly removing several weighty shampoo bottles, we found to our chagrin that we were still overweight. Even after the removal of several more weighty items, each suitcase was still right on the borderline. However, a gracious airline staff member took pity and let us pass this time.

In two hours the plane to Beijing was going to take off. We still had some time. This time, as before, I bought Dad a bowl of noodle soup at a food plaza near the boarding gate. He found some comfort in his airport Japanese noodle soup. Terry was having a cup of coffee while reading the Saturday edition of the *San Jose Mercury*. I got two cups of non-fat steamers and blueberry muffins for Celine and me, then we joined Dad and Terry eating at a table. While eating, Celine took her iPod from her Victoria Secret Pink bag and started surfing for her favorite songs, using the airport's free WiFi access. At a table to the right side of ours, a group of four college students was discussing something in a European-sounding language. Judging from their appearances and their backpacks, they could be those adventurers that I had often spotted in Yellowstone or Yosemite National Parks during our past camping trips. Where would the next stop be for those world travelers, I mused? A table on the left was occupied by an elderly Chinese couple. They were talking to a young lady holding a baby in her arms. I supposed the young woman could be their daughter and the baby might be their grandchild. As I was wondering about the couple, the lady, and the child, I heard slurping sounds from Dad's direction as he ate his hot noodle soup with great gusto.

"I think we will all be on the same plane to Beijing," Dad said to me looking at the elderly Chinese couple while eating.

"It would be nice if you get to know them. You will have someone to talk to on the plane. Do you want to ask them where they are from?" I said while examining the couple's faces.

"I will ask them once I pass the gate."

I often hear that once many young Chinese couples or exchange students come to this country, they apply for temporary U.S. visas for their parents in China so that the parents can also come and look after their grandchildren. If the parents' visas expire, they send their children back to China to live with their grandparents for a few years. I wonder how this works for the children and the parents. What does it mean to the child, parents, and grandparents? I can't imagine that I could ever do the same to my daughter. I would never wish to miss out on her precious, formative years of life. Decisions to send their children back to China must have been very tough for these young parents. What other choices did they have? They have to cope with the reality of a high cost of living, a fast paced society, and a stressful working environment in America at full steam. The pressure to succeed for these young people is too high in this country. As a result, they don't have enough time or energy to spend quality time with their children. They would have never sent their children far away if they had better choices.

Dad finally finished his noodle soup. He wiped his mouth and hands with a piece of white tissue, then stuffed another wad of tissues into his carry-on bag. "I will need it later," he said, as if there were no tissues available on the plane. Dad stared at the moving crowd in front of our table for a second, then turned around to Celine,

"Celine, you will have to learn Chinese."

"I will, I will," responded Celine, seeming to understand by telepathy and visual clues.

"You know, China will become the most powerful country in the world in the next decade.

There will be a future for you there," Dad said seriously.

"Yes, yes," Celine responded, this time responding to my translation of Dad's admonition.

"You should visit China, since I won't be back. There are so many changes in China.

Your brother also wishes to see you," Dad looked at me and said.

"I will, I will," I muttered.

I agreed without saying any words like "if" or "but". In the past I always tried to find some reasons to delay my next visit to China. I wished to make Dad happy this time. I didn't want to disagree with him, especially today. Dad seemed to be anxious while he was waiting to board. I sensed his determination to leave this country forever. My hope for him to return again was grim. A cloud of sadness filled in my heart and stabs of pain slowly crawled from the top of my head down to my toes at this moment. I was too weak to control my feelings. I hadn't felt this way for a long time, not since when my parents saw me off at the Beijing central train station before I left for Inner Mongolia in 1969. Just yesterday Dad and I were walking in our neighborhood after supper. I couldn't bear to think that there would never be another walk together in America.

In the past five years, Dad and I had become companions like never before. At the time, I either didn't pay any attention or thought to our activities together, or at the time, constantly struggled to make myself understood. This togetherness now would become a real treasure stored in my memory and buried in my heart forever. "It is time to go, Dad. It might take a while for you to negotiate the long line at the security check. You will have to take off your shoes when you go through," I said reluctantly to Dad. Terry grabbed Dad's carry-on bag; Celine took one of Dad's hands; I was clinging on one of his arms. We all started walking slowly to the check out gate. As Joseph John Campbell, an American mythologist once postulated, "Eternity isn't some later time. Eternity isn't a long time. Eternity has nothing to do with time. Eternity is that dimension of here and now which thinking and time cuts out. This is it. And if you don't get it here, you won't get it anywhere. And the experience of eternity right here and now is the function of life." I was feeling and smelling every second of Dad's presence. I was feeling my eternity with Dad at this very moment.

We were stopped by security at the end of a long waiting before the gate. My mind wasn't following the conversation that Dad, Celine, and Terry were engaged in. By the time I slipped out of my random thoughts, there were only two people ahead of us at the point where only those holding boarding passes could enter. It was time to say good-bye. I was all nerves and my heart was racing fast. My face might have been turning red, as I felt the heat radiating from my face and entire body. I gave Dad a firm hug then a quick peck on his cheek. I promised him that we wouldn't leave until we could no longer spot him in the security area. All of sudden it seemed that Dad didn't know how to be the center of attention. His body jerked back. There was an awkward grin on his weathered face. It was Dad's typical reaction that I had come to know since I was a child. What was he thinking at this moment? Did he feel the same parting sorrow as I did? Both Terry and Celine gave Dad a huge hug and said good-bye afterwards. Taking his carry-on bag from Terry's hand, Dad quickly turned away and walked straight to the gate. Dad's steps were slow but confident, and each step was a reminder that there would be no return. "Home is where the heart is". He was certain which direction he was going. Watching Dad's every step, I couldn't control my shaky emotions. "Mom, you must be very sad," Celine sputtered. "Yes. He is my dad. I love him. I don't know when I will see him again," I said painfully, with my eyes becoming misty. We stood outside the gate waiting and searching for Dad for at least ten minutes. Dad gradually disappeared in the crowd of travelers. In another fifteen hours he would be drinking his jasmine tea and enjoying a bowl of Chinese noodle soup in Beijing.

On the way back to our central California coastal home, I felt that half of my soul had parted with Dad. Although Dad and I differ in choosing our paths and destiny, our hearts and souls will always be connected. Dad isn't perfect and has his faults. Yet he is my hero. He is one of the *Giants in the Earth* as far as I am concerned. Dad has searched and found his role and place in Chinese society. "Follow your bliss," was Joseph Campbell's admonition. To Campbell, heroes "conveyed universal truths about one's personal self-discovery and self-transcendence, one's role in society, and the relation between the two". Dad has followed his bliss. His life experience in America was short, however this endurance enabled him to re-discover himself and his spirit. Although China, the place I once called "home sweet home", has changed dramatically, I haven't changed with it. It is within the context of North America, another continent, another culture, different from my ancestry, that I have changed. What is China now, and what lies in my future? Have I already reached my destination? In a way I have. I have a loving family and a comfortable home. I have been successful in my professional career and I am striving to do more for my professional community. I am willing to take on any projects that garner my interest and that can still challenge me. I cannot predict what lies in my future. One thing I am sure of is that I have not yet reached my final destination. There is no time to sit down and put my feet up. Life is still a long journey for me. I am on my way to continue my journey, a journey to discover and rediscover myself, to search for truth within the human spirit.

Bibliographies and Notes on Resources

CHAPTER TWO: LOVE HAD
EVERYTHING TO DO WITH IT

Page 17 - Page 18.

Turkenburg-van Diepen, Maria Gertrudis Wilhelmina. *Crystallographic Studies of Modified Insulin.* University of York, 1996.

Page 21.

"Chinese Zodiac: Your guide to Chinese Astrology: Chinese Zodiac - the Horse," *ChineseZodiac.com*, accessed February 9, 2011, http://www.chinesezodiac.com/.

CHAPTER THREE: ONE HUNDRED STEPS

Page 28.

Weinstein, Jay A. *Social and Cultural Change: Social Science for a Dynamic World.* Lanham, MD: Rowman & Littlefield, 2005.

Page 36.

Dainian Zhang and Ryden Edmund, *Key Concepts in Chinese Philosophy.* (New Haven, Conn: Yale University Press, 2002) 75.

CHAPTER FOUR: TO CAMP OR NOT TO CAMP

Page 43 - Page 44.

The Star Report, "Vatican among those not impressed by Avatar," *San Jose Mercury* (San Jose, CA), 2010.

Page 49.

"Yan'an - Symbol of the Chinese Revolution," *China.org.cn*, accessed February 9, 2011, http://www.china.org.cn/.

Page 51.

Yoshiko Nomura, *Lifelong Integrated Education as a Creator of the Future: the Principles of Nomura Lifelong Integrated Education 1.* (Stoke on Trent, England: Trentham Books for the Nomura Centre for Lifelong Integrated Education under the auspices of UNESCO, 1998), 105.

CHAPTER FIVE: BOWL OF NOODLES

Page 54 - Page 55.

"Chinese Noodles," *Wikipedia: The Free Encyclopedia*, last modified October 18 2012, http://en.wikipedia.org/wiki/Chinese_noodles.

Page 58.

"Chinese Noodles," *Museum of Learning: Explore a Virtual Museum of Knowledge*, last modified October

19 2012, http://www.museumstuff.com/learn/topics/
Chinese_noodles_history.

Page 62 - Page 63.

Solomon H. Katz and William Woys Weaver, eds.,
"Acceptance and Rejection," *Encyclopedia of Food
and Culture 1.* (New York: Scribner, 2003), http://
galenet.galegroup.com/servlet/eBooks?ste=22&docNum
=CX3403499999.

CHAPTER SEVEN: MONEY TREE

Page 81.

Ians, "China's president dons Mao suit for National Day,"
Online Latest News, last modified October 1, 2009, http://
www.latestnewsonline.net/.

CHAPTER EIGHT: CHILDBIRTH

Page 98.

"Natural Childbirth," *Wikipedia: The Free Encyclopedia*,
last modified October 12 2012, http://en.wikipedia.org/wiki/
Natural_childbirth.

Page 99.

B A. Hotelling, "Psychoprophylactic to Orgasmic Birth,"
The Journal of Perinatal Education 18 (2009): 45-48,
accessed August 10, 2012, doi: 10.1624/105812409X474708.

CHAPTER NINE: LITTLE EMPEROR AND LITTLE PRINCESS

Page 106.

Yunjie Cheng and Xiaojie Yu, "Oh, please. Give us a baby boy," *ShanghaiDaily.com* (Shanghai, China), Dec. 9, 2010.

Page 114.

Gopnik, Alison. *The Philosophical Baby: What Children's Minds Tell Us about Truth, Love, and the Meaning of Life.* New York: Farrar, Straus and Giroux, 2009.

Page 117.

Kimberly L. Keith, "Building Character - Child Development - The Eight-Year Old," *About.com Guide*, 2011, accessed February 9, 2011, http://beaguide.about.com/index. htm.

CHAPTER TWELVE: MARCHING WITH MAO

Page 155.

Mao, Zedong. *Selected Works of Mao Tse-tung.* Vol. 4. Peking: Foreign Languages Press, 1961.

Page 155 - Page 156.

English, Allan D. *The Changing Face of War Learning from History.* Montreal [Que.]: Published for the Royal Military College of Canada by McGill-Queen's University Press, 1998. http://site.ebrary.com/id/10132325.

Page 157.

Mao, Tse-tung. *Carry the Revolution Through to the End.* Peking: Foreign Languages Press, 1961.

CHAPTER THIRTEEN: 2008 OLYMPIC GAMES

Page 177.

The statistics on the numbers of athletes attending the 2008 Olympic Games and medal results are from *Beijing: Official Website of Beijing Organizing Committee for the Games of the XXIX Olympics* - August 8-24, 2008, http://en.beijing2008.cn/index.shtml. The quotation of "truly exceptional games" is from:
Alan Abrahamson, "Truly Exceptional Games," *NBCOlympics.com*, August 24, 2008, http://www.nbcolympics.com/index.html.

CHAPTER FIFTEEN: GOING HOME

Page 194.

Matthew Ciolek, "2004 Tsunami Disaster - Scholarly and Factual Analyses," *The World-Wide Web Virtual Library*, 2005, http://www.ciolek.com/wwwvlpages/asiapages/tsunami-analyses.html.

"Hamdan vs Rumsfeld: an Important Supreme Court Decision," *MultiEducator, Inc.* 1994, http://www.historycentral.com/Today/hamdan.html.

Page 194 - Page 195.

Elisabeth Rosenthal and Andrew C Revkin, "Science Panel Calls Global Warming 'Unequivocal'," *New York Times* (New York, NY), Feb. 3, 2007, accessed October 19, 2012, http://www.nytimes.com/2007/02/03/science/earth/03climate.html?pagewanted=all&_r=0

Page 200.

"Episode 2, Chapter 12: The Power of Myth," *BookRags. com: Research Anything*, 1999, accessed February 9, 2011, http://www.bookrags.com/.

Page 202.

"Joseph Campbell," *Encyclopædia Britannica Online* (Chicago: Encyclopaedia Britannica, 2011), http://www.britannica.com/EBchecked/topic/91229/Joseph-Campbell.

Acknowledgments

My deepest appreciation goes to a group of writers, colleagues, and friends including Nancy N. Chen, Debbie Jan, Bruce Finlayson, Terra Hangen, Constance Lim, Robert F. McEwen, and Irene Reti for their honest, thoughtful and valuable suggestions to nurture this book, that would have been impossible without their early votes of confidence. My warmest gratitude goes to Bernie Griffiths, Darby Li Po Price, Doug Stewart, and Judy Yung for their enthusiastic support and for nourishing my writing spirit. My special thanks go to Geoff Soch, Tim Lindsay and a team of brilliant and creative professionals at the FriesenPress. With their support, the book production process went smoothly and seemingly effortlessly. Finally to my family: Dad, thank you for your inspiration. Celine, thank you for your lovely smile and for your consistent encouragement. Terry, my rock, thank you very much for your kindness, wit, and guidance on all matters and for your believing in me when I didn't. You have endlessly edited and re-edited my manuscript a thousand times. I offer my love always and forever.

About the Author

Wei Wei is a Fellow of the Special Libraries Association and is the editor and co-editor of *Scholarly Communication in Science and Engineering Research in Higher Education*, 2002; and *Leadership and Management Principles in Libraries in Developing Countries*, 2004.